Million
Dollar
Closing
Techniques

Million Dollar Dollar

Closing Techniques

THE MILLION DOLLAR ROUND TABLE
CENTER FOR PRODUCTIVITY

JOHN WILEY & SONS, INC.

New York • Chichester • Weinheim • Brisbane • Singapore • Toronto

This book is printed on acid-free paper. ∞

Copyright © 1999 by The MDRT Center for Productivity. All rights reserved.

Published by John Wiley & Sons, Inc.

Published simultaneously in Canada.

This publication is designed to provide accurate and authoritative information in regard to the subject matter covered. It is sold with the understanding that the publisher is not engaged in rendering professional services. If professional advice or other expert assistance is required, the services of a competent professional person should be sought.

Designations used by companies to distinguish their products are often claimed as trademarks. In all instances where the author or publisher is aware of a claim, the product names appear in Initial Capital letters. Readers, however, should contact the appropriate companies for more complete information regarding trademarks and registration.

Library of Congress Cataloging-in-Publication Data:

Million dollar closing techniques / The Million Dollar Round Table
    Center for Productivity.
        p.   cm.
    Includes index.
    ISBN 0-471-32551-1 (paper : alk. paper)
    1. Selling. I. The Million Dollar Round Table (Park Ridge, Ill.).
    Center for Productivity.
    HF5438.25.M5687   1999
    658.85—dc21   99-22889

Printed in the United States of America.

10 9 8 7 6 5 4 3 2

CONTENTS

Chapter 4

Anticipating and Handling Objections   117

Chapter 5

Phrases That Will Help You Close   191

INTRODUCTION

The premise of this book is that you are already a sales professional, and now it's time to raise the bar. Why the title *Million Dollar Closing Techniques?* Simply because the core information you are about to read is directly culled from one the world's most prestigious sales organizations—the Million Dollar Round Table. But before getting to the details of selling, let's address the question: What is the Million Dollar Round Table?

In 1927, thirty-two sales professionals who sold life insurance gathered in Memphis, Tennessee, to share sales ideas. They expected that the synergy of the group would enhance the professional skills of each participant. Today, the objectives of that group have grown into an international organization of nearly 19,000 members in forty countries, and have expanded throughout the financial services spectrum.

The Million Dollar Round Table commands universal respect. From a humble beginning, it has grown into the premier sales organization in the world. What is the MDRT magic? Over a long period of time, it has developed a set of core values, and these values have bound this prestigious organization together, nourished and sustained it, and made it the great organization that it is today. What better way to introduce this book and what the MDRT is all about than to articulate a number of these values and suggest how they can be used to help you realize your full professional and human potential.

MDRT's most important value is *productivity,* on both a professional and a human level. The Round Table was founded on a level of production that set the highest standard in the sales field, and today it represents the top 6 percent of sales representatives in the world. Within the organization, there are two additional levels of productivity, at three times and six times the basic entry requirements. The philosophy of this prestigious sales organization is "Dream big dreams" and turn those dreams into reality.

In 1962, Dr. Mortimer Adler introduced the concept of human productivity to MDRT. Dr. Adler challenged MDRT members to understand the intrinsic need of all human beings—particularly successful human beings—and to reach both inside and outside themselves so that meaningful lives can be achieved for more people. Essentially, what Dr. Adler presented was an idea whose time had come for the Million Dollar Round Table. Its members had reached a point where they realized that sales success is not enough; life is more than the sum total of what a person does for a living. Who an individual is is more important than what an individual does. Dr. Adler said that some aspects of life allow a person to simply live, and other aspects permit a person to live well. The Round Table adopted what it now calls the Whole Person Concept, a balance of seven vital life parts: (1) health, (2) family, (3) spiritual, (4) education, (5) financial, (6) service, and (7) career. By definition, whole persons are engaged in a lifetime quest to achieve balance and congruity in all aspects of their lives and to continually seek the development of their full human potential.

Grant Taggart, a late Past President of MDRT, expressed the Whole Person Concept very well: "Personally, I believe in the acquisition of property and the making of money, but I contend such is not the all-important thing. Someone has said that, when you sum it all up, success isn't gold, it isn't in doing some deed that is bold. For the money we make or the houses we build mean nothing the moment one's voice has been stilled. But he or she has succeeded who, when he or she has gone, in the hearts of people is still living on." This philosophy has made MDRT sales professionals the successes they are today.

MDRT's *sharing and caring spirit* is a value that is cherished by its entire membership. Born at the original meeting in 1927, it has become a hallmark of the organization. The MDRT has a rich tradition of sharing knowledge for the benefit of its members, its clients, and its members' companies. Unselfish concern for each other reflects MDRT members' truly unique and positive quality.

Commitment to excellence is a value that pervades the organization as well. Nowhere is this value more evident than at the Annual Meeting, considered to be the finest sales meeting in the world. The greatest tribute paid to this meeting is that many MDRT members spend more than 10 percent of their annual income to attend it. As evidence of MDRT's commitment to excellence, more than 1,200 members actively serve the organization each year, and MDRT's professional staff is a model for other sales organizations around the world. Superior performance has become MDRT's minimum standard.

In 1969, Marshall Wolper, an MDRT member, gave MDRT a new value by challenging each of his MDRT associates to *"Always stay over your head."* His basic premise: Don't be afraid to try a new market because you have limited knowledge. One doesn't learn how to sail by reading a book. Jump in and give it your very best; you will learn by doing, and you will grow by working diligently in your new selling endeavors.

Dr. Alec McKenzie gave the organization an important value with his *time management* philosophy, "No one has enough time, but everyone has all there is." Through McKenzie, MDRT associates learned about time wasters and the importance of delegating tasks to others. When sales professionals practice time management, their time can be spent on doing the job they do best—meeting prospects and clients to uncover and then solve their problems. MDRT sales professionals are, first and foremost, problem solvers.

A reinforced value for MDRT members is the importance of *goal setting*. The members need to know what they want from their business and their personal lives, and then set their sights on achieving those goals. Goal setting gives sales professionals a track to run on and the ability to measure their progress. MDRT members have learned that they can achieve what their minds can conceive. They dream "big dreams" and then set their goals to realize those dreams.

The Million Dollar Round Table has stressed the value of *professionalism*—conducting oneself as a professional in all activities. New members can learn or enhance their professional skills. MDRT sales professionals firmly believe that they must be good at who they are and what they do.

Although many other values could be mentioned, the final one that should be highlighted is MDRT's emphasis that its members should take the high road and demonstrate, by their leadership, that it is not enough to do what is legal or even what is ethical. They must always choose to do what is right. They firmly believe that one need never be contrite for doing the right thing, and taking the high road in all facets of life is the right thing to do.

What does all this add up to? Quite simply, phenomenal closing success, and this closing success is transferred to you throughout the chapters ahead.

Chapter 1

What Is Closing?

Closing is anything that a sales professional does to cause a prospect to buy *now*. MDRT sales professionals look at closing in a number of different ways. It builds trust, it is the final process in a sales presentation, it educates, and it solves problems. But the secret is always the same: getting prospects to *want* to make a favorable decision. Let's begin by discussing an important factor in all closing opportunities—the exchange of trust between sales professionals and their prospects.

The sale is the result of a delicate and complex interplay between you and your prospect. It is delicate because it involves a keen and sensitive analysis of subtleties: What are the unspoken objections, and who is the real decision maker? It is complex; many interrelated technical and personal elements are involved: obvious and hidden costs, current and predicted economic conditions, and human feelings, thoughts and aspirations. Closing is an interplay between two or more people who are similar in many ways yet different in significant ways. You and your prospect enter the sales conversation with limited knowledge of each other, and with biases and preconceptions that may keep you from really understanding each other. On the other hand, the sales conversation may be the beginning of a long and mutually satisfying relationship.

This delicate and complex interplay may lead to the prospects' decision to buy (with significant benefit to you and your customer) or may instead channel the sale and commission to a previously uninvolved sales professional whom the client privately favors. Success or failure in any sales effort depends on many factors. One of the most profound and subtlest factors is the bridge of trust established in the relationship between you and your prospect.

The essence of a professional relationship is trust. We take the advice of a professional in law, accounting, medicine, or finance. We trust that it is in our best interest to do so. We go to a counselor for help and advice when we are in trouble, when we are in doubt about what we should do, or when we sense that our life would be enriched because of contact with a professional who cares about us. Professionals enjoy the highest respect because we believe we can trust them, depend on them, and obtain strength and courage from them.

Research shows that when two or more individuals are involved in problem-solving activity, the level of trust between them has a significant effect on the outcome. Where there is high trust, there will be a greater exchange of relevant ideas and feelings, and more clarification of problems and goals. There will also be more personal satisfaction with the problem-solving efforts, and more motivation to implement the conclusions. These research findings are directly applicable to business sales situations. Building a professional bridge of trust with prospects is an effective sales strategy.

Mutual Trust: An Essential Factor

Strategies for Building Trust

There are definite strategies for building trust. These strategies are effective in building trust in a marriage, in a parents-and-children relationship, in a business setting, and in professional counseling relationships. Choosing the correct strategy requires understanding the characteristics of trust:

- ✓ Trust is a feeling. It is fragile. It takes time and effort to build trust, but only an instant to destroy it.
- ✓ Trust comes in degrees. We may feel greater or lesser trust toward a particular person.
- ✓ Trust is situational. We trust a person in one situation more than in another.
- ✓ Trust depends on the task involved. We trust a person to do one thing, but not another.
- ✓ Trust depends on the time. We trust a person at one time more than at another.
- ✓ Trust depends on the other people involved. We trust one person or group more than another person or group.
- ✓ Trust is complicated. We may need to examine the issues involved in the delicate and very human activity of trying to build, or rebuild, trust in a world where levels of trust are not very high.

Begin with Yourself

The most fundamental strategy for building trust begins with ourselves. We cannot *make* others trust us. In fact, the more we try to convince others that they can trust us, the less likely they will. They may wonder, or even ask, "Why are you protesting so much?" It takes two people to form a sales relationship—(1) the sales professional and (2) the prospect—and neither has total control over the relationship or the final outcome of the sales effort. The sales professional only has control over himself or herself. But self-control is a powerful factor in any relationship.

We can start to build the level of trust by increasing the level of trust we feel in ourselves. What does it mean to trust ourselves? *Merriam Webster's Collegiate Dictionary,* Tenth Edition, defines trust as "assured reliance on the character, ability, strength, or truth of someone. . . ." To trust ourselves is to feel a degree of certainty that we will do what we think is the right thing to do. The definition of what is "right" is highly individualized. Does what we *think* is right become part of our own definition of trust? How do we implement this first strategy of building trust in a way that increases the feeling of trust in ourselves?

The answer is both simple and complicated. It is simple in that we need only make sure that our behavior is consistent with our basic values. It is complicated in that it takes effort and soul-searching to define and clarify what those values are. Values are personal qualities that we believe have worth. They may include principles of right and wrong, activities that we think are important and significant, and material possessions that we find highly desirable. It is common to value two things that are in conflict. When this occurs, it is almost impossible to behave in a way that is completely consistent with our entire system of values. Anyone who attempts to write down and define a set of personal values will discover potential value conflicts and will become aware of how difficult it is to resolve them. A person with a high degree of self-trust is likely to have the clearest concept of personal values and the most determination to live a life that is consistent with those values.

Sales professionals who have a high sense of trust in themselves will believe strongly in the value of the products and services they sell, and in the worth of seeking out those who need them. No one likes to be told "No" about something that is strongly felt, but self-trust will help a sales professional realize that the prospect who refuses an appointment or refuses to take needed action is the person with the problem. If the sales professional takes the refusal as a sign of personal inadequacy or inferiority, the sales professional has the problem.

A sales professional who has a high sense of trust will ask questions to determine directly who the decision maker will be. High trust will make it easier to deal with the vexing problem of another sales associate who may be close to the prospect but not visible in the selling situation. It is frustrating and costly to prepare a proposal for a prospect and then have the actual sale go to another sales associate who is favored by the prospect. Perhaps the most trusting and professional way to deal with this potential problem is to raise it directly with the prospect, early in the exploratory stage of the sales process.

Be Consistently Real

We tend to trust people who are consistent in their behavior. We can count on persons whose behavior is predictable. We are likely to be friends with people whose behavior is at least relatively predictable. Knowing where we stand with members of our family, or with colleagues in business, is a source of comfort; we can anticipate how they will react in most situations. But rigid consistency may not provide the flexibility needed to cope with our often changing and turbulent world. Carl Rogers, the internationally renowned psychologist and psychotherapist, believes that, in building a relationship of trust, being "consistently real" is more important than being rigidly consistent. Normal human beings experience swings in mood, changes in interest, and slow but inevitable modification of values as they progress through the stages of life. A consistently real person will acknowledge these changes and be open about them. The concept of openness is inseparable from the concept of trust. As Rogers says, integrity is "utter sincerity, honesty, and candor; avoidance of deception, expediency, artificiality, or shallowness of any kind." The true sales professional would hope to be viewed as a person of integrity; the practice that makes this more likely is appropriate self-disclosure.

Practice Appropriate Self-Disclosure

Self-disclosure is risky, but trust depends on it. The highest levels of trust appear to exist between people who are genuinely open about what they believe, value, and feel; but when they reveal personal aspects, they risk making themselves vulnerable. Others may not like what they hear and may reject the self-disclosing persons. We know that we cannot be all things to all people, nor is it desirable to try; we might wind up with no identity at all. On the other hand, it is unwise to "let it all hang out," or tell anything and everything about ourselves to anyone, regardless of the circumstances or situation. To be totally closed, or totally opened, is to be extreme and ineffective. A balance is needed, but how is it measured? Just how open or honest should we be? How much self-disclosure is appropriate if we want to develop the most effective professional relationships of trust?

Appropriate self-disclosure is a necessary ingredient of effective, high-trust, professional relationships. *Appropriate* refers to what is proper or suitable, given a particular situation. In business circumstances, the sales professional may approach the prospect either through a strong third-party referral or via a cold call. In the first instance, the sales professional will be "borrowing" on the prospect's trust in the referring person, and that trust is likely to be temporary. Even with a good referral from a trusted friend or associate, the prospect will quickly move into a test-and-search process to learn: "Can this strange sales professional really be trusted?" In a cold call, the sales professional will be dealing with whatever level of trust the prospect has for sales professionals in general.

If the prospect is a cold call, the sales professional is likely to have an uphill campaign. First, the sales professional must build sufficient trust for the prospect to reveal information that is necessary for the preparation of a sales proposal. Then he or she must further strengthen that trust or the prospect will reject the recommendation. Whatever the situation, appropriate self-disclosure by the sales professional will tend to increase the level of trust in the sales professional–prospect relationship.

What is *appropriate* self-disclosure? Common sense tells us that it would be inappropriate to bring up personal problems and anxieties associated with a sales professional's private life. Attention should stay focused on the problems and issues that are important in the prospect's life and business. But the sales professional remains a thinking, believing, feeling, and valuing person during the sales conversation. To attempt to hide all these aspects of the self would not only take effort but would be a form of deceit. Disclosing nothing about the self would be inappropriate, and an attempted cover-up of personal history probably would be detected by the prospect. Some advisers suggest imitating professional counselors who reveal nothing personal but probe and attempt to open up their clients to gain intimate knowledge of their values, feelings, aspirations, fears, goals, and objections (to the counselors' recommendations). A counselor may have learned that being "professional" in an interview means (1) being careful not to reveal any personal reactions, feelings, or judgments toward the client, and (2) maintaining a neutral or nonjudgmental attitude throughout the interview. This so-called clinical approach may be interpreted by the prospect or client as indifference or coldness. A more enlightened view would expect no greater degree of openness from the prospect than we are willing to risk for ourselves. Common sense also tells us that a person will speak more freely with another person who is obviously open or nondeceitful and who has little to hide.

In dealing with a business owner or a high-level manager in a corporation, the psychology of the sale is often similar to that of a personal sale to an individual. The decision-making process may depend heavily on the emotional impact or degree of empathy generated in the prospect relationship. In selling to a publicly-held corporation and dealing with professional managers, there is more questioning because of distrust, a less personal relationship between agent and prospect, and perhaps more emphasis on the numbers involved. But even in this situation, human beings are involved. Feelings do influence decision making, even if those feelings are not disclosed or acknowledged. The agent who is more open in that situation is likely to be more sensitive to the emotional factors and the numbers involved. Sales strategies are likely to be more effective when they are based on emotional as well as numerical information.

Practicing more emotional openness offers four distinct advantages to sales professionals, managers, parents, spouses, or anyone interested in increasing levels of trust in relationships. They will be: (1) more authentic, (2) more human, (3) models of coping behavior, and (4) persons with whom others will be more open.

To be authentic is to be "worthy of acceptance or belief as conforming to or based on fact," the dictionary tells us. Successful businesspeople are realists. They make excellent decisions based on fact, not hope. They have become sophisticated skeptics not just to be skeptical, but to have knowledge and awareness based on how things *are*. A typical business prospect has years of experience in trying to separate truth from fantasy and real people from phonies. These judgments are not always correct, but businesspeople are unlikely to be sold on a sales approach that is contrived and presented by a person who is attempting to display emotions that are not genuine, or pretending to have skills that are not possessed. A sales professional who shows more enthusiasm or more personal interest in the prospect than is felt is trying to build a relationship of trust on a base of deceit. Especially in a sales relationship that is likely to extend over a period of weeks, months, or years, sales professionals who have authenticity will have a higher probability of winning the client's confidence and retaining the account.

A degree of humanness is necessary in any professional to whom we turn when we are in need. Dehumanizing or mechanical approaches to people in management or sales—or in our families—lead not only to a lowering of trust, but also to lower levels of productivity and human growth. A manager, counselor, spouse, or parent experiences a whole range of feelings: self-doubt, self-confidence, depression, elation, confusion, certainty, and so on. People are different in some ways, but seem to be alike in many more ways. A personal relationship based on friendship or a professional relationship based on confidence seems to offer a perception of similar interests and values. What better way to establish a relationship than to have each person acknowledge basic human needs, feelings, and aspirations?

A sales professional can be a model of coping behavior for clients, colleagues, and family. We obtain strength and courage from such a model—especially when we can observe how the professional copes with stress or uncertainty. If the professional is low in self-disclosure, we will not recognize the coping skills that may be there. If, however, he or she is open about experiencing normal human stresses, frustrations, minor depressions, and confusions, we can see how these are dealt with successfully, and that lesson is of value to us.

Perhaps an even greater advantage of higher levels of self-disclosure is that they stimulate higher self-disclosure from others. In counseling, sales, or management, it is advantageous to be aware of the thoughts, feelings, and doubts of a client, prospect, or subordinate. We work better with people we know well. Highly self-disclosing professionals will find that people with whom they interact will tend to be more open in return.

The Importance of Being a Good Listener

The ability to listen well helps build a bridge of professional trust. Most of us are sensitive to when we are actively being listened to, and when the "listener" is merely pretending to listen. But what happens when two excellent listeners get involved in a conversation? If you are imagining a lot of silence taking place, you are visualizing poor listening. A good listener talks a lot about what the speaker has just said. A poor listener talks a lot, but may be changing the subject or roaming far from what the speaker has said or is feeling. A good listener listens to what is said, what is not said, what the speaker would like to say but does not know how, and what the speaker is feeling.

Professional listening helps build trust in four ways:

1. It emphasizes points the prospect or client is making.

2. It helps focus the conversation on important issues.

3. It encourages the speaker to reveal more of the aspirations and doubts that exist.

4. It demonstrates that the listener understands.

Good listening is not just repeating what the speaker has said, but it does include that. Excellent listening involves thinking of examples to illustrate what the speaker has been saying. The speaker may then say with delight, "Yes, that's exactly what I meant."

Listening creates the feedback needed to confirm that communication is taking place. There is nothing more disconcerting than talking to someone who maintains a poker face and does not even nod or say "Uh-huh" occasionally. A good listener has a responsive face; it registers the puzzlement, concern, delight, and enthusiasm of a genuine listener who is getting to know another human being. When a financial counselor meets a skeptical business or professional prospect, both have the task of understanding and learning from each other; this is a necessary process for effective problem solving. Ideally, both are good listeners, but the counselor must have real control over his or her listening ability. There is much evidence that an excellent listener, by example, will encourage better listening in others. Good listening enhances trust in a relationship.

Avoid a Stratagem

A stratagem is an artifice or trick to deceive or outwit an enemy. Shortly before D-Day in World War II, the Allies leaked false information to the enemy in an effort to divert some of the resistance from the planned invasion at Normandy. On a much lesser scale, people use stratagems to gain an advantage over other people, especially in adversarial relationships. We tell part of the truth, we flatter, we pretend, and we falsify when we try to dominate others or to be the winner in what we see as a win–lose situation. If the selling relationship is seen as adversarial by either the seller or the potential buyer, the stratagems will be part of the sellers "pitch" or the buyer's objections. If the selling relationship is seen as professional, or as a psychological partnership, then stratagems will interfere with the best possible outcomes because they will prevent high levels of trust from evolving as two or more people work together.

Develop the Capacity to Care

Not all people who work in caring professions really care about their clients or patients or students, but a great many people in all professions and areas of business do care about clients, customers, and the population in general. Is your business a caring profession? Perhaps you feel strongly that it is. Sales profession-als usually experience a renewal of faith in their profession when satisfied customers not only provide positive feedback but refer to their business to friends and associates.

To care is to be vulnerable. To avoid the pain of disappoint-ment and the anguish of rejection that accompany most human relationships, we would have to discontinue our psychological and emotional involvement with others. We may not experience discomfort, but we will not experience love and companionship either. Loneliness is like a disease; it reduces the quality of life for millions. All of us experience loneliness in some form occa-sionally, but overcoming it is largely under our individual con-trol. No one can reach out *for* us; we must do it ourselves. Love and caring are personal responses, and we individually create our internal levels of those feelings toward others.

Become a Model of Professional Trust

Trust is a feeling shared by two or more people and built more by example than words. Verbal efforts to assure others that we can be trusted may have the opposite effect. They may wonder why you're protesting so much. Trust is subtle and fragile. It grows slowly and may be destroyed at any moment. Trust is built by using strategies that are essentially ways of living. It is destroyed by using stratagems. Ralph Waldo Emerson reminds us: "What you are stands over you the while, and thunders so I cannot hear what you say to the contrary."

We do our part in building relationships of trust when we in-crease our trust in ourselves; when we are consistently real in disclosing who we are; when we listen; and when we avoid strat-agems and develop the capacity to care. All of these contribu-tions to trust are under our control and can become part of our way of life. We convey trust more by being someone than by saying something. We can think of trust as a fund of resources to be spent in a relationship, an organization, a nation, and the world. We might increasingly make deposits to that fund through our example and the degree of openness we allow ourselves. By making trust deposits, we add to our personal growth. When we withdraw from that fund of trust, we leave it and ourselves impoverished.

Membership in the MDRT suggests leadership beyond the number of dollars involved. It states that leadership has already been acquired and its full potential is yet to be reached. Effective leadership involves delegation of many things, but trust is not one of them. We cannot delegate trust; we must model it every day. When we minimize our concern for ourselves and maximize our concern for others, we endorse a principle of human growth and we exhibit our personal approach to building bridges of trust. This is our ultimate responsibility toward ourselves and those whose lives we touch.

Close It But Don't End It

No aspect of selling has been as completely misunderstood and shamefully neglected as the closing. Sales professionals who have focused their attention on getting acquainted, on finding a favorable atmosphere for a sale, or on following up leads and having an enviable familiarity with the problems of their prospects, have often stumbled into failure because they did not understand the meaning of the closing. Sales professionals who have generated admirable enthusiasm for their products have been unable to translate their inspiration into sales because they did not know how to add the finishing touches of a strong closing.

What is a closing? For too many businesspeople, it is the striking of appropriate keys on a cash register, a pleasant smile, and a "thank you" as a package or receipt is placed in the hands of a waiting customer. To others, it is a form letter that thanks a buyer for an order, before turning to new prospects, new orders, and new closings. Or it may mean placing a signature on a contract—a legal requirement and nothing more. To these people, closing is a brief moment. The most tenuous of threads connect it with the interview that has preceded, and with the relationship and future sales that should follow. In other words, these sales professionals consider a closing an ending.

But closing is not the end or the beginning. It is a climax in a continuous process. Why struggle to become acquainted with customers' needs, problems, and economic positions so that only the shortsighted goal of closing a single sale is accomplished? The final goal—the really worthwhile goal—is to win a permanent customer who brings in consistent sales.

Whether the product being sold is something as intangible as an insurance plan or as real as a glittering diamond, the psychology of closing scarcely varies. In the body of the interview, the sale is promoted through a combination of solid logical arguments and reasons to have confidence in the sales professionals and everything they represent—a company, a product, a trademark, and their own integrity. Every logical argument is advanced to establish and close the sale.

But logic alone is not enough; logic stimulates only thought. Proceed on the theory that emotions stimulate action. Digging deep into the wallet is a step that requires an emotional stimulus. The feeling of pleasure derived from satisfying a need or simply obtaining something new must be greater than the difficulty that we all feel—even the most generous giver or the most notorious spendthrift among us—as we sign a check or part with hard-earned cash and all the security it supposedly represents.

"Appeal to the hearts of prospects as well as to their minds." This guiding motto will see you through many years of hard and tough selling. Whenever possible, appeal to prospects' hearts by linking the sale with the happiness of a spouse or a child. Nothing melts the resistance of buyers as quickly as the suggestion of how the loved ones in their life will enjoy and appreciate the purchase of the product under consideration.

The following example, narrated by an MDRT sales professional, illustrates how you can use this type of appeal in your own selling. It requires little imagination to understand that similar appeals are applicable in any other field of selling. This experience can be applied to almost any situation where one person is attempting to use his or her persuasive powers to convince another to take some action. Selling is merely an effort to persuade another person to buy an idea, a thought, a product, or a service.

In the very early days of my group insurance activities, I was having lunch at a favorite rendezvous with a man who had just become vice president of a rather prominent firm. Through years of persevering struggle, he had worked his way up to a position of eminence in his industry, and was still climbing. However, he seemed deeply perturbed that day, and upon questioning him I learned that he had had an unpleasant and disturbing experience just before leaving for New York the previous afternoon.

A week earlier, one of the firm's employees, a man in his late thirties who had been working for the firm for over fifteen years, had died. Without warning, he had been snatched away from his wife and children. There had never been any intimation of poor health. Like many other wage earners who look forward to years of life and work, he had saved little and had invested hardly a penny in insurance.

Here, sitting with me, was a man as sympathetic and humane as any who could occupy a chair in an executive's office. Deeply interested in every employee in his enterprise, he had known John well. They had smiled to each other with "Good Morning" almost daily over a period of years, had stopped to chat about production problems in John's department, had exchanged best wishes alongside the company's Christmas tree in one holiday season after another.

And then John was ill and, a day later, dead; and my companion was grieving deeply over the tragic and untimely loss. A few days after the funeral—the afternoon before our meeting in New York, in fact—John's widow had come to my friend's office. She was obviously unprepared to carry the burden of being mother, breadwinner, and widow.

She came to explain her position: she was left practically penniless, and her children were too young to allow her to go to work. She had no parents or in-laws to whom to turn. "John worked for you all these years," she pleaded. "Surely you owe him something—some help. You can't let his family lie down and die. He was a trusted employee; he worked hard for this company, defended it as if it were his very own, if anyone dared to breathe a word against it. Even when he took sick, awakening with a headache or a cold, he always went to work—he felt he owed this to you." On and on this continued, until it reached the inevitable: "You're not going to let us down, are you?"

On the other side of the desk, my friend had sat and listened. And he had answered that appeal with help, although he knew that the aid extended was far from adequate, and knew, too, that it was not a sound financial policy for a company to solve a problem of this sort in an individual, almost haphazard manner.

As I listened to this story, I realized that one could not hope for a more favorable atmosphere for consummating a sale. What more would be needed than to show the client that there is one, and only one, answer to a situation like this? Nothing can alleviate the grief of the young widow, or of the children who must face the future years of life without a father. However, the very real physical hardships may be reduced by a far-sighted insurance plan.

In this instance, the emotional appeal had already been made for the sales professional. The logic of cold argument was to come later.

Now let's reverse the roles and draw from a sales professional's experience as an impartial observer at a sale. A friend of this sales professional was going to buy a new car, and invited him to come along. The friend had a pretty good idea of the price range he could manage, had heard the usual conflicting reports about the relative merits of the various makes and models, and finally took the step of walking into the local showroom of one of the leading car manufacturers. A sales professional, almost as shining and dazzling as the cars around him, walked up and engaged the two friends in conversation.

During the early part of his monologue, the car sales associate concentrated on the advantages offered by the manufacturer whose car he was selling. He discussed some of the safety devices in highly technical language, thus flattering the prospective buyer by assuming he understood them; he explained fluid drive, power steering, springs that cushion the shocks from the bumps in the road, and the mileage obtained per gallon of gas, as compared with other cars of equal weight.

The impressive arguments were based on good sales psychology; not only was the buildup of logic convincing, but there was little opportunity for rebuttal. Even if there were errors in what was being said, this sales professional was unlikely to encounter customers so familiar with features of new automobiles that they could raise serious objections.

And then, subtly and gradually, the tenor of his sales arguments began to undergo a change. The appeal to reason, he must have figured, had been successful. Next, an appeal to the emotions. The brain was won; the heart was waiting patiently to be conquered. "You have a wife?" he asked, and when the client answered in the affirmative, he spoke glowingly of the pride of ownership, the convenience the car would offer, and the feeling of good grooming and success the owner would experience when he pulled up in front of a country club in this vehicle.

"Would you like to surprise her by driving up to your home in the car," he asked, "or would you prefer to have her come in and help you make the final choice?" Sales resistance was dropping to a new low! The friend said that his wife preferred being in on the buying rather than being surprised with an accomplished deal. The sales professional followed that tack with remarkable persistence. He might be able to reach the wife by telephone; if so, he could have someone pick her up and bring her right over to the showroom. In fact, they could do a demonstration drive at the same time.

No sooner said than done. Before long, the wife was riding over in the car that her husband was already almost committed to buy. In the meantime, pending her arrival, the sales talk continued; but it had again shifted in emphasis. The deal was deep into closing, and the observer could recognize a technique that he himself had frequently used: "Not whether, but which."

In the moments of culminating a sale, when the last element of resistance appears to be disappearing, there should be a change in the emphasis of the interview. No longer is the customer to be presented with a "yes-or-no" choice. No longer is it a question of whether the customer wishes to buy. An assumption is made that the customer *will buy, from you, now.* The customer is therefore asked: "Which one do you prefer?" and is given a choice of colors, of price ranges, and of styles—depending on the nature of the product or service being sold. The shift from *whether* to *which* takes place almost imperceptibly. The query is not which one will be bought, but which one is preferred. Even when a very large variety of choices is available, only a limited few are offered because too many choices will lead to confusion and may postpone, if not entirely kill, the budding sale.

As he eyed the attractive dashboard, the observer recognized the "Not whether, but which" technique that was so much a part of his own selling philosophy. "Which color do you like best?" he was being asked (not "Which color are you going to buy?"). The form of the question could not possibly repel customers, or even put them on guard. People have preferences, but as soon as they state their preference, they have moved much closer to committing themselves to the purchase. A preference for a black car was finally expressed; it was almost implied that a black car should be set aside. By the time the wife arrived, the husband was bubbling over with enthusiasm, and, given their similar tastes, they soon agreed to purchase the car. The sale was made and a binding check was signed and delivered. The man and his wife were pleased with their new car, and his friend was happy to have been an observer at such an excellent closing.

Another story centers on a sales executive in a wholesale firm that sells ladies' handbags. This woman is fortunate in having an excellent product: the handbags are among the best that are made. If you could eavesdrop at one of her presentations to an important out-of-town buyer, you would observe a master sales professional at work.

First, she resorts to logic. She exhibits the whole line and carefully points out the special features, advantages, superior craftsmanship, and style of each bag. Then, taking into consideration the buyer's market—what size town he comes from, what clientele he has—she selects the type of bag she thinks his customers would find most attractive.

She shows the buyer that the handbags are roomy without being bulky. Then she calls attention to the smooth, hardy, long-lasting leather on the outside, and the durable and fine materials that have been used within the bags. The safety feature that prevents accidental opening is demonstrated. Gradually, the conversation is shifted from the practical to the aesthetic aspects—the equivalent of the change from logic to emotion. "This is a model for people to admire—one that is useful both in business and when going out; one that will complement any color ensemble and will be appropriate with a suit as well as with a dress."

Finally, approaching a climax to the sale, she glides into the closing, smoothly working in her own version of "Not whether, but which." The exact nature of her closing is, of course, dependent on the course the sales interview has taken until that point. "Do you like the rectangular one or do you think the square bag is smarter?" she may ask the buyer, or she may give a choice between a smaller and a larger bag, suggesting that the smaller one may be better if only the most essential needs are to be carried.

As we leave this sales professional to close her sale, it's appropriate to state basic principles and definitions. A closing is the action individuals take to commit themselves—almost beyond recall—to the purchase of an article or service. In the insurance business, it is the process of signing an application and giving a binding check. In a department store, it may involve signing a sales slip and showing a store charge account number; or it may be effected merely by saying, "I'll take this one," and producing cash or a credit card.

Up to the point of closing, the seller and prospect have been talking about something that is needed. Now, action is taken. Once the sale is made, reversible action is not impossible, but relatively few sales are lost after a closing. If individuals change their minds, the goods and services not yet received can usually be canceled. Even those delivered can sometimes be returned, but such action is relatively rare. Stores that facilitate the return of merchandise actually receive back a very small percentage of all the goods shipped from any one department or in any one period of time.

The closing is the step taken by buyers to implement and legalize a sale. It is an affirmative and positive step. People who like to talk, or have a need to procrastinate, or thrive on discussions and investigations, find any closing distasteful. They do not like to take steps that commit them to anything, especially a binding contract or an expenditure of funds. They may like something, they may want it, and they may even be "sold on it," but their minds keep searching for new exits so that they will not be forced to embark on a program of action.

Such people raise objection after objection, but their objections are only camouflage. Without ever attempting to railroad anyone into a sale, and without giving an impression that the customer cannot retreat and reconsider, sales professionals must get a decision so that they can go on to their next opportunity.

"I *can* take no for an answer," such a customer must be told. Realizing that the sales professional is no longer willing to tolerate procrastination, the customer will either pick up a pen and sign the agreement or put an end to the interview.

If, by that time, the selling has been accomplished properly, the prospect will realize that a refusal will be a greater loss to self than to the sales professional, and the closing will be made. To back this point, let's review the story of a great sales professional who, many years ago, failed to close a sale—after the customer had said "Yes." The sales professional was Jules Gleason, who at one time was a high-ranking executive of Cartier's, the celebrated store that handles millions of dollars' worth of jewelry each year. When he was a young man, selling in Cartier's Paris store, he was sent to meet an Indian maharajah who wanted a sapphire ring. Gleason had such a ring to sell: its oval 150-carat stone was worth $40,000, and the ring had once been among the crown jewels of France. He arrived at the hotel where the maharajah was awaiting him, displayed the stone to the Indian potentate and his companion (an appraiser), and awaited their decision while they spoke to each other in their own language. They then stated that His Royal Highness would purchase the ring. Gleason immediately started to quote the price, but he was summarily interrupted. The ruler would take the ring, he was told. Price was not to be mentioned.

At this point, Gleason volunteered a little extra information. He told the interpreter that the ruler might like to know that this ring had once been worn by Louis XIV of France. The information was given to the maharajah, who, after a moment's reflection, made a curt remark to his companion. The latter translated: "The order is canceled."

Jules Gleason looked up, dismayed, and asked why the maharajah had changed his mind. He was informed that His Highness did not want his head chopped off! When he returned to the store to report his failure, Pierre Cartier told the young man that if he had remembered to point out that the ring had once belonged to "the great Louis XIV," he would doubtless have made the sale!

Close of the Sale: A Permanent Relationship

There are no secrets to effecting a close. Although much has been written about the existence of a mystique or a sequence of miraculous activities that sets the close apart from the rest of the sales process, this slant is patently untrue. Actually, the success of your efforts at the close will be directly proportional to the soundness with which you have built the foundation for a complete sale.

Your sales presentation must be made in terms of your prospects' interests. Their desire must be aroused and their conviction secured through proper handling of any objections. Closing techniques can be applied with assurance and effect only after these stages have been covered.

A sale cannot be closed if the other stages in the selling process have not been completed. A solid foundation, composed of an honest value story that satisfies customers' wants and needs, makes the close possible. The close does not evolve from the sales professional's manipulating strings so that the buyer does the sales professional's bidding; it is the logical culmination of all that has happened since the beginning of the sales encounter.

Sales professionals direct their efforts toward helping buyers resolve to make the purchase. They realize that any individual who must express a preference for one item over another is making a decision. Such a decision goes beyond just selecting one product over another from among a group of competitors. The product must compete with all others, in every industry, for the consumer's dollars. In accepting one product, consumers must forgo others. This is why buyers move reluctantly toward the close of the sale and the moment of decision.

The Many Psychological Moments

Experienced sales professionals put their stress on an adequate sales story before they use any of the closing techniques; they know that this is the only "secret" to successful closes. They also know that many "psychological moments"—not just one—are available to them for closing a sale. This is why they try to close from the moment that they believe the prospect has received an adequate sales story. Experience has taught them that prospects will usually provide certain indications that they are ready for the close, and these indications occasionally take the form of some physical action. Prospects who have been listening quietly to a presentation may nod their heads in agreement with some particular sales point, or they may reach again for a sample that they looked at earlier.

Sometimes, an emphasis on a genuine objection is the green signal that tells you the prospect is ready. There may be a serious question about a guarantee offered by your company, or about whether the product will do exactly what the manufacturer is claiming. A customer, in voicing an objection, is saying, "Answer this and I'm going to buy." A statement by a prospect—"I think this feature is best," or "This seems to be the best line of hardware on the market"—is his or her closing signal.

Naturally, sales professionals have a variety of trial closes. Remember, trial closes are designed to help you smoke out a prospect's mental reservations. These techniques will often point the way, but the green light that says, "Close now!" is something you must learn to see through experience. You will often find it flashing more than once—with some "caution" signals in between.

Assurance and expectation should characterize your attitude toward the close. Your every word and action should convey the complete confidence you have in the outcome: a closed sale to another satisfied customer. When that attitude is conveyed to the prospects, it helps to dispel any doubt they may have harbored. Confidence, like enthusiasm, is contagious, so look, feel, and think like a sales professional, *a person who makes sales.*

Your attitude is also important because it determines the income you will receive and the profit your company will realize. Regardless of what you may have done to develop the prospect's interest, there is no commercial value unless the sale that is closed satisfies your customer's interest, the order is sent in and filled, and the payment is collected. By definition, a successful sales professional is a reliable closer.

Techniques for Closing Sales

The techniques you use in the close are your own choice. Creative selling does not permit a "prescription approach"—an attempt to pigeonhole each prospect as a certain type for whom only one rigidly followed technique will work. Sales professionals should be conditioned to be flexible and adaptable. They might fruitfully combine two or more of these techniques. Their final choice of a single closing technique or a combination will be determined by the facts of the sale and the personality of the prospect with whom they are dealing.

Among the techniques used most often to close a sale are:

- ✓ Presumption technique.
- ✓ Choice technique.
- ✓ Inciter technique.
- ✓ Ask-for-the-Order technique.
- ✓ Report technique.
- ✓ Comparison and contrast technique.

Presumption Technique

With this technique, you imply that you absolutely believe that your prospect will buy the item being sold; there is not a shadow of a doubt in your own mind that a sale is pending. You are so certain the major buying question has been settled that you perform an act (such as writing up the invoice) that must be stopped by the prospect if the close is to be postponed. Success in the use of this technique is founded on your own positive feelings of confidence. Your presentation pictures your prospect already in possession of the product.

The following scenario depicts how this technique is illustrated. The office manager of a small manufacturing company has been looking at a floor model of a specific copy machine in a sales professional's showroom. During the discussion, the sales professional established the advantage of the low cost of making copies on any kind of paper, from ordinary bond to fine stationery. He had learned from their discussion that the prospect had an immediate need for a copier that would produce copies that would be impossible to distinguish from the originals. Here is their dialogue in addressing their respective concerns:

SALES PROFESSIONAL: "... and this copier will provide such rich detail that you will have to look several times to see if they are not really originals."

PROSPECT: "Well, I was kind of worrying about the...."

SALES PROFESSIONAL: "You mentioned earlier that you had some special copying jobs to get out. Let me see if I can arrange to get the machine here on Monday. I'll call my office now."

The sales professional moves toward the telephone and knows that the sale is closed because an action has been performed that the prospect did not interrupt. To halt the sale, the prospect would have had to stop the sales professional from making the call.

A variation of the presumption technique uses a series of affirmative decisions by the customer to secure the order. In the following exchange regarding a real estate transaction, these favorable decisions are made as the sale progresses.

SALES PROFESSIONAL: "With a growing family like yours, I'll bet these three bedrooms are appealing to you, aren't they?"

PROSPECT: "Yes, and we may be needing four not too long from now...."

SALES PROFESSIONAL: ". . . and did you ever see a better place to add a fourth than that northeast wall, adjoining the bathroom?"

PROSPECT'S SPOUSE: "Just think, this kitchen is bigger than the living room of our apartment!"

PROSPECT: "That may be so, but at least our landlord pays for the heat now. The furnace here is going to eat up oil!"

SALES PROFESSIONAL: "Well, of course, you're going to have to spend money to heat, but the small extra cost of heating will more than be justified by the increase in living space for your growing family."

PROSPECT'S SPOUSE: "What's that?"

SALES PROFESSIONAL: "The isolation of the sleeping area from the living room—not so much chance to get on each other's nerves as there is in an apartment. And you haven't overlooked the fact that the house itself is separated from other houses and from the street. Your kids are at their most active now, aren't they?"

PROSPECT: "They sure are. They can use the space on this corner lot."

PROSPECT'S SPOUSE: "And ask their friends over without disturbing."

SALES PROFESSIONAL: "Well, tell me frankly, have we looked at anything else that's better—for your family?"

PROSPECT: "This does look like the pick of the lot. . . ."

SALES PROFESSIONAL: "It wouldn't surprise me if some others thought so too . . . but I do know that you can hold it now with your deposit. Let's get back to the office now and make the arrangements."

These are excellent closing techniques to use if an honest and sincere presentation has been made. They make it difficult for the customers to refuse to buy. The prospects above have been placed in a position where to say no would contradict all of the features they have been looking for in a house.

Choice Technique

One of the most widely used methods of closing is the choice technique, which closes the sale on a minor aspect of the product or service. Sales professionals avoid the major buying decision by having their customers make their selection on the basis of a minor or secondary point. The technique's effectiveness is acclaimed by most experienced and successful sales professionals. The prospects always make their choice from among the various products that have been presented—their ultimate choice is never between buying or not buying the product. Whatever the decision of the customer, the result is always the same: a sale.

As simple as this technique is, skill is required for its successful use. Never try to rush a customer with it, and be certain that the choice you offer is the correct one. The technique can be effectively used to test your progress toward the close. Most importantly, it can leave you no worse off than if you had not tried to close. If the customer is not ready to buy, you can resume your sales presentation and, at another propitious moment, try again. If the customer is ready to accept your proposition, the answer to your question on choice will, in effect, give approval to your proposition.

The following questions illustrate various uses of this technique:

✓ "Do you prefer the two-door model in blue, or did you like the red one better?"

✓ "Would you like to use our deferred payment plan, or would you prefer to pay cash for your purchase?"

✓ "Is it convenient for you to take this with you, or shall we deliver it on Saturday?"

✓ "Which finish do you prefer, the rough or the smooth?"

✓ "Would you prefer an IBM computer or a Macintosh?"

✓ "Do you wish wall-to-wall carpeting, or the new area rug?"

✓ "Is it more convenient to schedule delivery in this month, or early next month?"

Used with tact, this method can only enhance your sales presentation. It can produce positive results if you are certain that your prospect is close to a favorable decision.

Inciter Technique

With a little practice, this relatively easy method will serve you exceptionally well. It should, however, be regarded as a last-resort tactic. The inciter or incentive urges and impels the prospect to act at once. It may be an offer of an easy payment plan, a worthwhile free gift to the prospect, prompt delivery, or some other feature that encourages the prospect to act immediately. The sales professional's efforts are directed at preventing the prospect from putting off until tomorrow, or any future date, a purchase that should be acted on now. Some sales professionals use this technique where a final, powerful extra reason is required to impel the buyer to act.

The technique has great effect, largely because of the entirely natural desire to get something extraordinary at no extra cost. In addition, the technique addresses itself to the drive, in almost all individuals, to protect what they already have and to avoid losing something of value that they possess. People will go to great lengths to hold on to what they have. Note carefully, in the following dialogue, how the inciter contributes to closing the sale because the sales professional keeps stressing a theme of "Protect what you have."

[The house that the paint salesperson is visiting needs decorating inside and a full exterior painting. The imminent result of further neglect will be rapid deterioration of the entire house. The prospect is trying to procrastinate.]

SALES PROFESSIONAL: "This house you own must represent a large investment."

PROSPECT: "It certainly does. But what with the taxes, interest, and insurance on it, I don't want to put any more money into it right now."

SALES PROFESSIONAL: "To delay painting now means that you will have to wait until next spring to. . . ."

PROSPECT: "I'm still going to wait! I've got plenty of other things to do with my money."

SALES PROFESSIONAL: "Sure, but you know what the severe winters in this area can do to a frame house that isn't properly painted. Enough damage was done last year by the freezing rains and heavy snows."

PROSPECT: "Last winter was a severe one, but it didn't do any damage I can. . . ."

SALES PROFESSIONAL: "Notice? That's just the point—the elements do their damage underneath, where you can't see it."

PROSPECT: "It can't be that much, or it would have pushed through."

SALES PROFESSIONAL: "That's the trouble! It gives no warning—just comes through completely and then the damage is really done."

PROSPECT: "Well, I still think I might wait another year."

SALES PROFESSIONAL: "That's up to you now. Just let me say this: You may suffer a double loss by waiting. First, you will probably have a major repair bill, far in excess of what it could cost to do the job now; second, you will have permitted your investment to depreciate."

PROSPECT: "Well . . . I sure wouldn't. . . ."

SALES PROFESSIONAL: "You can prevent both losses. Let's see what we can do to keep your home in the condition you really want. We can give it the protection that will maintain its value for years to come, and, at the same time, save you a costly repair bill next year."

A word of warning: Use this sales tool *only* if it is forged in truth and based on genuine facts. Only an unscrupulous individual would apply such a device if the impending event or condition were not going to occur.

In a variation of this method, the sales professional might describe a situation in which certain consequences are highly probable—for example, a change in prices—based on past experience. The sales professional must be sincere in the prediction and would be well advised to state clearly that probabilities, not facts, are involved—lest the future confidence of the prospect becomes forfeited. Any sales professional who wants to build a permanent career should not violate this trust.

Ask-for-the-Order Technique

This technique does not in any way humble or demean the sales professional who uses it. You need have no sense of inferiority when you make it work for you as a closing strategy. However, you still can't say to the prospect, "Please give me the order."

By using the approaches listed below, you ask prospective buyers to accept your proposition. You invite them to buy what you have for sale. When other methods have not succeeded, your best strategy, always, is to ask for the order. The customers will in no way feel that you are begging. They will be impressed with your sincere determination to serve them—but only use this method for occasions that demand it.

- ✓ "Then I'll reserve 500 for you."
- ✓ "Will you take six this week?"
- ✓ "How about my sending a trial order?"
- ✓ "Why not give me your deposit now and be sure?"
- ✓ "May I have your initial payment now?"
- ✓ "Shall I write up your order now?"

Many prospects will not buy unless you do exactly what this technique suggests: Ask them for their order. You, as a sales professional, came to get an order; therefore, it is perfectly natural to ask for it.

Report Technique

To use this technique, you must relate an occurrence or story that in some way parallels your prospect's situation. Choose an anecdote or incident that permits you to draw an analogy to the circumstances of the customer you are trying to sell to; create a word picture of how another customer, in similar circumstances, benefited from your product or service. Then apply the lesson learned to the present prospect, and make an effort to close. Simply tell an old-fashioned success story that is intended to convince your customers of the merits of your proposal.

PROSPECT: "What you say sounds very good, but. . . ."

SALES PROFESSIONAL: "[Prospect's Name], you're acquainted with the Andrew Company, aren't you?"

PROSPECT: "Yes, I am. Usually run into some of their people at the convention."

SALES PROFESSIONAL: "It's a pretty good outfit, isn't it?"

PROSPECT: "Well, it's pretty common knowledge they have one of the shrewdest management organizations in the business."

SALES PROFESSIONAL: "They had an inspection problem, too, of a type very similar to yours. Well, they've licked it, and without hiring any additional help. Fact of the matter is, they are using fewer personnel for the inspection task than ever before."

PROSPECT: "How did they do that?"

SALES PROFESSIONAL: "With the same method I've outlined to you. Here's the story. Incidentally, they gave me permission to tell it. The same test I described to you earlier in our discussion conclusively proved to them that the solution to the inspection problem, where close tolerances must be maintained in a production operation—the same problem you are facing with a different product—was the application of quality control standards. The results were so outstanding they are going to install these methods in three of their other operations. . . ."

PROSPECT: "The results were that good?"

SALES PROFESSIONAL: "They certainly were; their rejections were reduced to the absolute minimum; customer complaints due to delays and bad production runs were eliminated. Naturally, their profit position has been substantially improved."

PROSPECT: "It sounds like it could be the answer."

SALES PROFESSIONAL: "Based on all our experience, I know that once the installation is made in your operation, your principal regret will be that you didn't do it years ago."

If you have documentary evidence for your statements, so much the better. The technique is especially effective if you can put the individuals concerned into direct contact with each other. But be careful: Customers often do not wish to have their names, or any information about their activities, used for private reasons. Be certain to maintain any trust given to you, and never accidentally disclose confidential information. To do so violates the ethics of professional selling.

Comparison and Contrast Technique

This is one of the finest methods of clarifying and emphasizing what you have been trying to demonstrate. It is effective because prospects understand new facts much more readily when they can be compared with or contrasted to familiar ones. Remember that a good comparison requires exactness and vividness. The strength of this technique rests on your carefully pointing out to your prospects how the product or service that you represent is the best one for them.

This is no time to knock your competition. Customers do not buy because somebody else has an inferior product; they buy because they have been shown that one product—your product—is better than any others. It will never hurt to admit that your competitor has a good product, but always show that your product or service is superior for the customer's purposes. Summarize your product's features, and emphasize the benefits to the customer. This summary method can be used to advantage at any time.

Find out what the sales professionals who represent your competition are saying about their products, and what features they are stressing. This may require real initiative and serious study, but your efforts will be rewarded many times over. Armed with this knowledge, you will have absolute confidence in your ability to make comparisons with your competitors and to emphasize the contrast between your product and theirs.

This technique is carried to its ultimate conclusion by a summarization of the features of your product as you approach the close of the sale. You know that when your prospects make their decisions, they are going to engage in a mental weighing of the pros and cons of a proposition, so why not help them as they do this?

Top Sales Professionals Are Closers

These various techniques have been tested and used by successful sales professionals. Your success with them will depend on your belief that you can attempt to close every prospect upon whom you call. No one with practical experience in selling will expect every call to result in a sale. The important thing is: Keep your attitude positive. Combine it with customer and product knowledge. Provide a value-packed presentation keyed to your customer's basic motivations and objectives, and you will succeed in selling.

Study and practice these techniques carefully; they will serve you well. It is mandatory that each one be mastered through practice and then proven through experience. This is the road to becoming a good closer.

After you close a sale, use the few remaining minutes of your interview to ensure your sale remains closed. Express your appreciation for the order and compliment the customers on the wisdom of their decision. Assure them of your continuing interest and your willingness to serve them regularly. While you are packing your samples or rearranging your portfolio, strengthen the sales professional–customer relationship by pointing out the personal wisdom they have just exhibited.

When You Fail to Close the Sale

Every interview will not result in a sale. But even a sale that is not closed can be made to work for you. You can accomplish this by sound merchandising. Indicate to prospects that you are always ready to serve them whether they buy from you or not. Make every effort to set the stage effectively for you to call on them in the future. Always "keep the door open" for a future visit. Every prospect respects an individual who can merchandise a disappointment. Goodwill—the most precious commodity that sales professionals and their companies can possess—is built on a constructive and positive attitude.

Good selling is based on the concept of helping every prospect and customer to buy wisely. This type of selling also guarantees a future for you. As a creative sales professional, your objective is always to provide your customers with satisfaction in your products and service.

Chapter 2

Preparing to Close

During the sales process, everything a sales professional does contributes to a successful close. Beginning with the initial interview, the salesperson gains a better understanding of the prospect, the prospect's style, and the prospect's motivations. Preparing to close means gradually creating an urgency to buy. It also means having a desire to prospect continually and to overcome any emotional barriers that prohibit you from selling your products and services.

The Seven Fundamental Rules of Closing a Sale

In 1959, Vince Lombardi, who is now memorialized in the Football Hall of Fame, took over as head coach of the Green Bay Packers. Lombardi had never been a head coach and the Packers were a losing team, but they were professional football players, so most coaches would have assumed they knew the basics of the game. Not Lombardi. He didn't say much during the first few days of practice. Finally, he called the team to gather around him, stood in the middle, held up a football, and said: "Gentlemen, this is a football." Remember, these were professional football players, and here was this short guy from the Bronx telling them: "This is a football!" Lombardi, who may well have been the best football coach ever, stuck with the basics. He never got fancy. By the way, when Lombardi said, "This is a football," one of the linemen, Max McGee, replied: "Coach, can you go a little slower?"

In October 1987, the Wall Street stock market fell 508 points in one day. Many people vowed to never again believe those articles about a 22-year-old who was born to be a financial genius because his investments turned back $40 million in two years. Many investors said to their mirrors, "I'm a jerk. I've been investing for years, and I'm not even close to my desired goals and probably never will get close."

Don't stop daring to dream. Dream of owning all the things you want, but remember that—in sales and in the rest of life—you won't reach those dreams by finding a magic formula to beat the system. Do the basics and do them well; they work. There are no magic formulas, no geniuses-from-birth, and no natural salespeople. Some people have more aptitude than others, but there are few "naturals." One of them was Wolfgang Amadeus Mozart. He composed his first symphony at the age of 10 and continued to write glorious music until his death. But being a natural isn't all it's cracked up to be. Mozart left us some great music, but he didn't have a happy life. He died in his mid-thirties, broke.

People who aren't naturals still dare to dream the great dreams, but they have to earn those dreams one at a time. In 1965, an extraordinary man named Richard Feynman won the Nobel Prize for Physics. He left his home in California and went to Stockholm to be awarded his Nobel prize. On the way back, he stopped at the high school he had attended, in the borough of Queens, in New York City. After he spoke to the school's students in the auditorium, he and his wife went to the principal's office, where Feynman's high school grades had been unearthed from the files. As his wife later reported the scene to the press, Feynman was surprised that his grades weren't nearly as high as he had remembered them. Then they showed him his IQ. It was 135. In most walks of life, that's a handsome IQ, but among physicists it is barely entry level. The reporters asked his wife if Feynman was devastated that his IQ was only 135. She said: "Oh no, he was delighted. He said to me, 'Darling, in the circles in which I travel, winning a Nobel Prize for Physics really isn't that big a deal, but to do it with a 135 IQ—that's something!'" People do reach their dreams the basic way: one step at a time.

You may ask, "How do I sell things that are perhaps out of favor?" That's a hard task. Your best starting point is to stick with the basics!

Here are the seven basic rules of closing a sale:

1. *Establish your credibility.* Credibility creates a favorable framework within which you can more easily make a sale. When you are credible, people listen. When they are confident that you know the answers, they don't ask as many questions.

2. *Know your product.* That doesn't mean spending your life as a researcher so that you know every last detail. It means knowing the risks and benefits of what you are selling and distinguishing people who should buy it from those who shouldn't.

3. *Know your client.* Listen to people, with your head and with your heart. Don't just wait for them to finish so that you can talk. Listen, and hear what they need and want.

4. *Keep it simple.* Always remember that the orator who was invited to give the Gettysburg Address was not the speaker most people would name today. It was a man named Edward Everett, and he spoke for an hour and a half. President Lincoln had been asked to simply say a few words to

close the program. He wrote and delivered a talk in which 75 percent of the words had five or fewer letters. He kept it simple.

5. *Sell concepts and benefits.* Disclose the facts and figures but sell concepts and benefits. Don't mislead your prospects into believing your products and services are something they are not.

6. *Communicate your enthusiasm, your certainty, and your commitment.* When you are selling, a lot of technical information must be communicated head to head. But that's not where sales are made. Sales happen below the neck—in the heart or in the stomach. And they happen as a function of your communication, your enthusiasm, your certainty about your product, and your commitment to your prospects.

7. *Take a chance.* You can take changes in a lot of ways, but focus on one: Stop asking for orders. Asking is a lot better than explaining and waiting, which is how many sales professionals start out, but it's not sufficient anymore. No matter what you are selling, your clients can go somewhere else and buy something that at least looks like it and is probably cheaper. Instead, be aware that every time your prospects turn on the television, pick up a newspaper, or go online via computer, they are given alternatives for spending their money. So much information and so many alternatives are now available that most prospects are confused and can't make a decision. A favorite close in the financial industry is: "What do you think?" Are you going to ask somebody who is confused what he or she thinks? Your prospects need you more than they've ever needed you, but they don't need you to ask them anything. They need you to tell them what to do.

Become a Doctor of Sales

It stands to reason that, given these seven rules of selling, the finest salespeople follow them. Who are the finest salespeople in our society? Among individuals, sales professionals are great, but among groups, medical doctors leave all others far behind.

Medical doctors tell you what to do and you do it. Have you ever asked your doctor—after he or she has written out a prescription for erythromycin—for some other "mycin?" Of course not! When your doctor tells you what to do, you do it.

Ever hear the following objection? Usually, it's not said aloud, but it is there: "I've decided to use you as my sales professional, but before we start working together, there's one thing I want to make clear between us, so that you know that I know. I can never totally rely on your recommendations. After all, you're paid a percentage as commission!" Doctors don't have this problem. They tell us what to do and we do it.

Why? Because they've set up the whole game that way. You're the biggest sales professional around. Everybody comes to you. But when it is time to see a doctor, you go to the doctor. And if you're like the typical professional person, you show up a few minutes early for your 11 o'clock appointment. The first thing you see in the reception area is the clouded sliding-glass window. You tap on the window lightly, like you're in a library, and a charm-school-trained receptionist throws open the window and says, "Can I help you?" You say, "I'm [Your Name] and I am here for my 11 o'clock appointment!" She reaches for a form, a clipboard, and a pencil, shoves them in your face, and says, "Sit down and fill this out!" You normally don't let people talk to you that way, but this is a doctor's domain so you fill it out. Many people who are new in sales are embarrassed when they must ask for personal financial information. How much money you made last year is not personal. The doctor's form—that's personal. But this is a doctor, so you fill it out, hand it in at 11 o'clock, and go right in to see the doctor, right? Some doctors set up their workday that way, but more often you'll wait about 45 minutes before you are ushered into the doctor's office. You sit there alone for another 10 minutes, and then the doctor comes in. He or she sits down and asks you more questions. For anyone else, you wouldn't answer some of those questions, but this is a doctor. Then the doctor puts down his or her pencil and nonchalantly says, "Go in the other room and take off your clothes!" You're not indiscriminate about where you take off your clothes, but this is a doctor's office. So you take off your clothes, wrap yourself in the paper "gown," and sit there alone until you are thoroughly chilled. Then, the other door to the room opens up and in comes a big, burly physician's assistant. This is not the little snip sitting out front; this is a big, burly woman in white. She positions herself between you and your clothes, looks down at her clipboard and says, "How are you paying for this?" Now that's closing!

Finally, the doctor comes in carrying a little metal instrument that he keeps in a deep freeze, and he puts that thing in places where a cold metal instrument doesn't belong—but this is a doctor. And when the doctor tells you what to do, you do it. Why? Because doctors, more than any other group in society, follow the rules of selling. They have established their credibility. They know their product. They know your body better than you know your body, or at least you think they do. And they listen; they have a stethoscope in their ears, and they listen. Doctors keep it simple. Ask a doctor too many questions, and he or she will say, "I'm sorry, I can't explain it to you; you don't have the background!" Doctors sell concepts and benefits, the classic example of which is: "Do it or die!"

Here's what a doctor *doesn't* tell you when he or she is selling you an operation.

At 6:00 A.M. on the day of your operation, a nurse of the op-posite sex will barge into your room and awaken you. He or she will then proceed to shave you in places that you would rather not be shaved by anybody, let alone a member of the op-posite sex. And he or she will do it much faster than you want. Then, before you recover from that shock, you will be placed on a stretcher and wheeled down the hall backward—it's al-ways backward—and you'll see these lights flashing by. Then, you'll go through some swinging doors that will go *bomp, bomp, bomp!* Finally, you will be in the operating room, lying under an enormous light. A mask will then be put over your face; you'll start getting woozy. As you drift off, we will be standing around talking about baseball scores. Then, as soon as you're out, we'll pull back your sheet, pull up your gown, and then take this knife, and we're going to do this, and this, and this, and then we'll pull your skin back and take your liver out and put it on the table, go get some coffee, and come back! They don't tell you any of that, and only rarely do they talk about price: "Excuse me, your pancreas is a little behind your liver. We didn't expect that. That will be an extra $450!"

Doctors communicate their enthusiasm, their certainty, and their commitment, not necessarily as to your chances for good health, but as to the fact that you are better off with them than you are with anybody else. If you don't believe they hold that stance, ask them how they feel about chiropractors. It's a little too easy to get laughs at the expense of the medical profession. After all, you might have some doctors as clients. But doctors are an extraordinary group of people from whom sales professionals can learn something about selling.

In sales, you deal with other people's money and you don't want to make mistakes. But sooner or later, most sales profes-sionals will make mistakes, particularly if they sell products that have a risk element. It's tough to face clients, and yourself, in that situation. If you make a mistake, remember what doctors do in the same circumstances: They recommend another course of treatment. And that's what you should do: Recommend another strategy.

Doctors take chances. They tell us what to do when we are ill, even when they are not sure of the outcome. They know that if they suggest or "sort of" recommend a course of treatment, we won't do it. So, even in the face of an uncertain diagnosis and the threat of a malpractice suit, doctors have the courage and professionalism to tell their patients what to do. Doctors take chances. They have the courage and the professionalism to tell their clients what to do in matters of life and death. If you want your doctor clients to respect you, and if you want your other clients to respect you the way they do their doctors, do what the doctors do. Follow these seven rules of selling, and tell your clients what to do. Be, if you will, doctors of sales.

Closing Starts with Goals

You've heard it a million times: "If you don't have a track to run on, you'll never get to your destination." You probably know that goal setting is your road map to success.

Why is it that you hear this again and again, time after time, from the most successful sales professionals, and yet the majority of sales professionals have no goals or plan of attack?

Why is it that you can go to an industry conference, hear superstars speak, concur with everything they say during their speeches, leave the conference inspired and fired up, and a week later not have implemented a single idea that was presented? Why is it that when you survey the people in your industry, only the goal-oriented segment is at the top of the heap?

Why is it that although some intensive studies have shown a direct correlation between goal setting and success, most of your peers in your industry don't set any goals?

Some of these questions may seem simple to answer; however, answering them is much more complex than it appears. This section suggests some ideas pertaining to goal setting and its importance. These ideas aren't new. Sales professionals have heard them many times in the past.

Why are goals necessary? Because goals give you a track to run on. Think of yourself in this scene: You are on a bike team in college and are confronted with a big hill. You're at the bottom looking up at the top, and climbing it seems almost impossible. However, if you identify a number of benchmarks, such as signs, trees, and telephone poles, and consider each benchmark a goal, your trip to the top is much easier. Do the same with your sales career. You want to get to the top, or peak, of your career, whatever you have ascertained that to be. As you sit at your present level and look up toward the level you want to attain, it looks difficult or even impossible to achieve. But if you set certain benchmarks along the road, your peak becomes much more attainable.

This same approach can help with what you need to do in the short term to reach you long-term expectations. By breaking your climb into the smallest possible increments and not deviating from your path, you should reach the peak in an efficient and timely manner.

It's not hard to realize why goal setting is necessary, but where do you begin? There are two perspectives for goal setting. The first is for sales professionals just beginning their careers; the second is for veteran sales professionals who have heard numerous times about the importance of goal setting yet have never taken that first step.

Newcomers probably have an easier time because their goals are usually set by a manager or mentor in the business. At this stage, the goal itself is not as important as the breakdown of the daily activity necessary to accomplish the goal. That is why a newcomer in the industry should set his or her daily goals and realize, from day one, that compromising them leads to failure. One MDRT associate related this personal experience in regard to this point:

> In my fourth year of college at Indiana University, we started our career interviewing process. Indiana, being a great business school, has all the Fortune 500 companies come to the campus to interview graduating seniors. We could sign up for these interviews on a first-come, first-served basis. The insurance companies came also, and we would interview with them to refine our interviewing techniques for the other interviews. Well, I did meet one insurance company that I was very interested in. I had some offers from major classical marketing firms and some from insurance companies. I discussed it with my parents and others, and they all thought I would be nuts to go with an insurance company after four years of college. So I took a job in a sales capacity and progressed rapidly into sales management. The whole time, I stayed in contact with the local insurance manager.
>
> I still was fascinated with this industry and eventually accepted a job in the business, to the dismay of many friends and relatives. My manager told me that all I need to do to succeed in this business is to persevere and have 15 appointments before I left Friday evening. If I didn't have 15, I should stay Friday evening and come in Saturday and Sunday. Well, I did this and was able to make MDRT my first six months in the business. He ingrained in me that activity was the key ingredient to success and never to compromise my goals. To this day, I still have activity-oriented goals, and if I don't meet those, I do come in on Saturday and Sunday to achieve them.

For some sales professionals, their biggest fear in life is fear of their power of rationalization. In every aspect of life, it seems, we can rationalize our activities. When we constantly rationalize negative activities, we soon can get far off our path and not even realize we've deviated from it. That is the prime reason for some of the statistics you see in the sales professions. For example, only 3 percent of the population can retire comfortably or are financially independent at age 65. In the financial industry, where sales professionals use this statistic every day in presentations, this same 3 percent relationship is common. The presenters tell their clients, "These people didn't plan to fail, they failed to plan."

For a veteran sales professional who has always understood the need for goals but has never set up a plan, goal setting is more difficult. The simplest way to do it is to analyze the five-year production results. Most goals are financially related, so the new goal for production might increase by some base amount or percentage—for example, 10 percent for the next year.

In your five-year review of your past production, if you have kept detailed records, you should try to determine the value of one set-up appointment. When you have done this, use a mathematical equation to break down the activity needed to achieve your goals annually, monthly, and daily.

Have these goals written and, as is strongly recommended, let your spouse, family members, friends, and/or business associates know what they are. By doing so, you create more incentive to accomplish your goals. Many people don't tell others about their goals because they fear they won't accomplish them.

After you have set your goals, how should you evaluate your progress? Activity breeds success, so you should have in your mind a set number of the prospecting appointments you need each week. Whatever that number is, make it a benchmark. You know you must have that number before closing your door for the weekend. Even though activity breeds success, you still must monitor your financial goals and break them down to dollars per week in commissions.

This can be done by creating a monthly log-in sheet that lists revenues received, cumulative revenues for the month, remaining dollars to reach the goal, and remaining percentage of time left in the month. This one page can, at any given point, give you a breakdown of where you are in relation to your goal.

Your monthly results should be logged in on a similar form that represents your annual goal. This sheet will be slightly different in that it also includes the prior year's monthly and cumulative annual results. This let's you compare the current and the prior year.

These simple log sheets are enough to let you evaluate how your year is going. It is also very important to reward yourself for reaching certain benchmarks along your road to success. Take a short vacation upon achieving your annual goal, or make a small purchase after realizing one of your interim goals. By accomplishing and rewarding one benchmark at a time, it becomes easy to climb to the top of the hill.

If there is one simple point that needs to be delivered, it is the importance of realizing that once these goals are set, they are set in stone and there is no compromising them. Do not give in to your powers of rationalization, or they could take over your life.

Building the Right Attitude

The close begins (and too often ends) with selecting the prospect and planning a sales presentation around that specific prospect's problems, objectives, and needs. The importance of this part of the job is obvious and the task itself may seem simple, but it can be deceptive.

One MDRT sales professional stated: "I never undertake a serious discussion of the products I sell with any person until I'm satisfied with the answers that I have to two questions: 'What will the effect on the prospect be if he or she does not buy the product I am recommending?' and 'What will the effect on the prospect be if the product is purchased?' This means that I have to know a great deal about my prospect before I make any attempt to sell."

He added that sometimes he could get everything he needed from a newspaper item, a credit report, a five-minute visit with some mutual friend, or possibly a short talk with one of his prospect's competitors. "But," he added, "usually, getting the kind and amount of information about people that makes me determined to go in and sell them takes a lot of time and a great deal of patient digging. For me, this has been a necessary investment—for if I don't know enough about prospects to get really excited about their needs for my products and services, it's likely that I may be eased out the door."

The sales professional who goes to the interview with a specific answer to a problem that is of real importance to the prospect is in a position not unlike that of a physician who has examined a patient and knows, as a result of observation and tests, exactly what that patient has to do in order to live a normal, healthy life. The physician will have no hesitancy in laying out the program that must be followed and will not be the least impressed with the patient's excuses for skipping or postponing the difficult parts of the program.

Because there is no vestige of doubt in the physician's own mind about what should be done, the recommendations will usually be accepted. The key here, of course, is the extent of the physician's diagnosis and his or her belief in the findings.

Sales professionals who approach their prospects' problems in the same way will develop an attitude not unlike a doctor's, and it can have similar influence on the prospects' reception of their recommendations. These sales professionals will be persistent (they will probably get more excuses than a doctor hears, so they'll have to be persistent), but their persistence of purpose will be based on exact knowledge, not on stubbornness or overanxiety to sell.

Much of the mystery, and perhaps some of the difficulty, surrounding the close disappears when sales professionals are fully prepared for the selling interview. It is also helpful to have and to keep a clear understanding of why most prospects object to buying now.

Almost every person who buys your products and services has a choice between investing in what you are offering, or using the same money for some other purpose. Successful sales professionals seldom have too much difficulty getting agreement that their products are important (especially if a product is recommended to meet a specific and recognized need). But convincing prospects that your products or services are important to them today, *right now,* is frequently anything but easy. Quite often, your products or services are for future delivery—yet they must be paid for with money in hand.

The prospects' probable responses are understandable. It *would* be nice to purchase what you have to offer. But maybe it's not an immediate need, so why get excited now?

It's a fair question. Why, indeed? Answer it by bringing the future into the present, and do it with enough conviction to excite the prospect about it now. But if you aren't sincerely concerned about a particular prospect's future, this may be a real chore. It may even be impossible.

A sales professional who knows the situation, and is concerned about it, usually has an advantage. There is no need to finesse this sales professional's attempts to close. The prospect, knowing that the sales professional is there to sell a particular product or service, fully expects to be asked to buy. So, when the sales professional starts asking closing questions, the prospect will probably offer objections, or try to dodge the issues entirely, or exhibit a lack of interest—but at least the prospect isn't going to faint from shock.

Some sales efforts are a lot easier. One supervisor was working with a new sales associate who went through an entire presentation without a single objection being raised. On every point, the prospect nodded agreement. When the presentation was completed and the prospect still said nothing, the sales professional turned to the supervisor and asked, "What do I do now?" The supervisor countered, "Get out your closing papers and start having the prospect fill them out!"

A sales professional's first objective, then, is to get the prospect's problem out in the open so that it is fully recognized and clearly understood. The purpose is to gain the prospect's confidence, not to force a decision. Realization of this basic fact has been a lifesaver to many sales veterans. It has helped them to relax and to be natural.

However, a sales professional who has established a prospect's need is at the place where the sale is made or lost. The sales professional should be thinking: "Am I beginning to feel sorry for this prospect? Do I feel that possibly the budget problems *are* as unique and as distressing as the prospect says they are? Am I beginning to agree with the prospect's reasons for not wanting to buy today—right now?" If the answer is "Yes," the sales professional is heading into serious trouble. If the diagnosis of the prospect's problem is accurate and the solution is sound, then the sales professional must know (and should not forget) that the longer action is put off, the more difficult the sale will become. Like a physician, a sales professional has a mission: Effect a cure; don't pamper or sympathize.

Again, if the sales professional's recommendations are sound, the prospect can nearly always find ways to accept them immediately—if the desire is there. The only safe rule, therefore, is to show no sympathy toward the prospect. The sales professional's attitude should be: "I'm sorry, [Prospect's Name], but this is your problem, and the longer you put off solving it, the more difficult it's going to be."

Is the close a separate part of the interview? A very natural question at this point is: "What is the cue that the interview has ended and that it is time to start the close?"

If there is any formal break between the interview and the close, it is what is called the silent period. This occurs when the sales professional has made the presentation and has answered the prospect's questions. At this point, the prospect might be thinking and will not say anything for a while. The sales professional should not disturb this silence—it's the prospect's time for wrestling with the problem. This silence might seem to last interminably, but sooner or later the prospect will say something—maybe ask a question or raise some minor objection. The sales professional should give a decisive answer and start to close the sale.

The advice to start completing the paperwork is quite important. It assumes consent and is probably the strongest close a sales professional can use. The reasons for this opinion will be discussed shortly.

The interview and the close cannot be regarded as two separate steps. Other than the aforementioned silent period, there should be no obvious break between the interview and the close.

When a row of dominoes is properly set up on a table, you can touch the first domino and, one by one in a continuous motion, the entire row will fall. That image of a continuous and uninterrupted procedure should represent the interview to the sales professional. Like a short story, there is a beginning, a middle, and an end; but if it is well written, the reader will not be conscious of where the middle starts or the end begins. Similarly, the entire sales interview should carry a considerable part of the closing load. The close begins with the approach, when the sales professional introduces the problem and emphasizes its importance to the prospect. If the problem is clear and important enough, and a solution is offered, the close is apt to be almost automatic.

There could still be objections or attempts to postpone action—those reactions, too, are automatic. But when the close is thought of as a part of the total sales process—something gradually built up through the interview—it becomes a normal, natural, almost inevitable climax to the interview.

Building the close on the broad foundation of the interview has another great advantage. There is less risk that the sales professional's closing attempts will be reduced to a weak, often offensive, and nearly always unorganized battle for the prospect's signature.

The Psychology of Closing Sales

✓ Do you feel you're sufficiently motivated and have enough drive and energy to earn even more than you are currently earning?

✓ Do you have your goals clearly targeted toward the specific end results you want to accomplish from selling your services or products?

✓ Do you feel you already possess enough talent and ability to be doing even better in sales than you are today?

✓ Do you feel you have the intelligence and knowledge to go to even greater heights of success?

✓ Do you feel you possess the necessary sales skills to achieve unlimited success?

✓ Do you feel you're empathic, sensitive, and ethical in dealing with your customers and their needs and problems?

Based on your answers to these questions, do you feel you're currently earning what you're worth? If you answered "Yes" to all these queries, congratulations! Your career is set!

If you didn't answer "Yes," then the key questions are: Why do so many talented, capable, ambitious people fail to earn what they're worth? What happens to all that talent, ambition, drive, energy, and knowledge? Somewhere along the line, it gets short-circuited before it reaches its goal.

It's time to destroy some age-old myths and develop a clear understanding of how and why the short-circuiting happens. What follows is the foundation for understanding the sales process, and a process for destroying myths and closing more sales. We begin by looking at five "selling realities."

1. *New prospects are the lifeblood of a sales professional.* Do you have any difficulty with this reality? To survive and flourish as companies and as individuals, sales associates must continuously replenish their supply of prospects. You must see those new prospects and ask them to buy.

2. *Selling is a numbers game.* The more buyers you contact, the more you close. Many sales professionals wish it wasn't this way. A quality game would be much more preferable.

3. *Without new prospects, all presenting and closing skills are worthless.* What value is there in knowing a lot and being adept at presenting your knowledge, if you have no one to talk to?

4. *Getting sales professionals to fulfill a schedule of prospecting, rather than showing them how to prospect, is sales management's greatest challenge.* All sales professionals must be taught how to prospect, how to make appointments, and so on. The challenge is in getting them to do it. If you're in management today, you realize the difficulty in finding people who will do this in sufficient numbers. In fact, industry statistics show that 80 percent of the people entering the sales field today will fail or quit within 12 months. New, excited, talented, motivated people who are ready to make a career of selling are falling out rapidly. That trend doesn't have to continue.

Are existing sales veterans immune to these bouts with low productivity, anxiety, or the possibility of quitting? Each year, 40 percent of the veteran sales professionals report one or more episodes of call reluctance severe enough to threaten their careers. This percentage represents only those willing to self-disclose. The true statistic is believed to be even higher. Many sales associates, if asked, would deny they have this problem, which brings us to the last selling reality.

5. *Assessment of the existing willingness or reluctance to prospect is the starting point.* You must be willing to ask yourself this question: "Am I call-reluctant?" Why is this important? What is the benefit of putting yourself through this process? For a barrier to be broken or for an increase in production to be achieved, you must see where you are today. You must take a realistic look and find out what's getting in your way, and proceed from there. Denying or ignoring problems or barriers will not eliminate them. Facing them and challenging them gets you to the starting gate.

At an industry conference not long ago, Norman Levine, a legendary MDRT sales professional, concluded: "The greatest challenge facing the sales profession today is the lack of prospecting." What is one of the key ingredients to attaining top productivity levels? Seeing more quality prospects more often.

George Dudley and Shannon Goodson, authors of *The Psychology of Call Reluctance,* are the leading researchers on call reluctance. In their 1988 landmark research project with MDRT, they found that Top of the Table sales associates were, without a doubt, less call-reluctant than others in the life insurance business.

To gain a clear understanding of call reluctance, let's provide this definition: Call reluctance is an emotional short circuit in a motivated, goal-directed sales professional. It reduces or eliminates the individual's ability to prospect on a consistent basis.

Understanding what call reluctance really is can help you destroy some age-old myths about a sales professional's main barriers to prospecting. For years, call reluctance has been labeled as the "fear of rejection" or the "fear of failure." These statements are far too general and ambiguous to be of any help in overcoming call reluctance. How do you remedy these fears? How have we been told to correct these two maladies? In times now past, the answer was: Just accept the rejection and go on. Often, sales professionals were exhorted with statements like, "If you really loved this business, you wouldn't let those things bother you." Did those cures work? No, because these myths aren't the true robbers of productivity. Call reluctance is more than a transfer of failing to call prospects. As the definition says, it is an emotional short circuit in a motivated, goal-focused individual.

You must assume that sales professionals have the motivation necessary to sustain a career, the energy to get the job done, and the drive and desire to succeed. You also should assume that sales professionals have clearly targeted, focused-on-the-end results they wish to accomplish from the use of their energy. If either of these two elements is missing, you are dealing with a different dimension of low production, and you can label these barriers as the "impostors" of call reluctance. They are just as career destroying and income robbing, but they require different methods of exorcism.

Call reluctance comes from learned behaviors that human beings are susceptible to. Three sources contribute to call reluctance: (1) personality predispositions, (2) heredity influences, and (3) exposure to other call-reluctant people. As a result of these three sources, the majority of people in sales today are not enjoying the success they so richly deserve.

How is call reluctance disguised? How do people cope with it? Following are characterizations of eleven types of people afflicted by call reluctance. Take a look at yourself and at people you know well. Have they earned these descriptives?

1. *Doomsayers.* Doomsayers are individuals who invoke worst-case scenarios. An example would be a thought like this: "If I call this person, I know for a fact that his company is already doing business with someone else, so there's absolutely no reason to even try"; or "If I got lucky and did actually sell this product, chances are the corporate office would turn down the loan. So why even try?" Doomsayers are highly self-controlled and have difficulty taking social risks.

2. *Overpreparers.* These individuals cope with call reluctance by overanalyzing and not taking action. They are very encyclopedic. Other sales professionals continually seek out the overpreparers for answers they should be finding themselves. Overpreparers spend countless hours doing documentation exercises; they look for the perfect solution to every problem instead of seeking people who could benefit from this knowledge. They continually seek information, at the expense of the prospecting process. They will never reach the true level of success that their preparation deserves. Unfortunately, many sales professionals are overpreparers.

3. *Hyperpros.* Hyperprofessionals invest their energy in *image.* "Do I have on the right attire to make this call?" Any activity that they perceive as demeaning or diminishing their professional stature is out of the question. Prospecting is seen as an act of hustling, a process detrimental to their credibility.

Hyperpros can be heard saying, "If they really want to do business with me, they can find me. Everyone knows who I am." They would rather be right than rich. They want to be seen as professionals, but they refuse to do what truly successful sales professionals do—see a lot of quality prospects, on a frequent rotation of visits. As production goes up, the hyperpro tendency diminishes dramatically.

4. *Stage fright sufferers.* These individuals dread giving group presentations. They feel very uncomfortable in front of any number of people they perceive to be a group; it could be 3 or 50. When opportunities to promote themselves occur, these people find excuses not to make the presentations. If forced to give a group talk, they read prepared notes verbatim. When given the chance to make their competence known before a group of prospects, they refuse. Their behavior is the opposite of good productive selling.

5. *Separationists.* Separationists are unable to mix business with friendships. They feel a friendship would be threatened by the intrusion of a business deal, and they say that they don't want to "use" their friends to get ahead or be seen as needing friendships to "make it" in the sales business. Networking is "out of the question." Asking for referrals from friends is "unprofessional." All those great untapped contacts go to other sales professionals who are willing to mix business with friendship. Many sales professionals struggle with this problem.

6. *Role accepters.* This type of call reluctance is a very curious malady. Those afflicted with it secretly dread being perceived as "involved in sales." They feel somewhat ashamed of their profession. To cope with this dark side, they use deflected identities such as "planner" or "consultant." The term "sales professional" is not in their vocabulary. Somehow, somewhere along the way, some significant other expressed strong disapproval of this person's being a salesperson. At every chance to sell or self-promote, this person hides what he or she does for a living, leaving thousands of dollars of commissions out of reach. The difficulty is *not* ignorance of what to say or how to say it, but a refusal to address prospective clients who are going to buy products from someone, someday.

7. *Yielders.* Yielders are wonderful, warm, enthusiastic people who do not want to be seen as pushy, forward, or intrusive. Yielders continually wait for the right time, the right circumstance, and a guarantee that they will not be intruding on others. They hesitate when it's time to close because of their self-imposed barriers of perfect timing. They shy away from confrontations. They never produce at the full level of their capabilities because of these beliefs. This type of call reluctance is moderately easy to cure because yielders take direction well and follow through on commitments. As production goes up, the yielder tendency goes down.

8. *Socially self-conscious.* Socially self-conscious call reluctance is target marketing in reverse. Socially self-conscious sales professionals refuse to call on the upscale prospects from whom the big sales originate. They are intimidated by people of prestige and wealth. They constantly shoot at the wrong targets because the people who have the power to make a decision on a large proposal are out of their comfort zone.

9. *Emotionally unemancipated.* Emotionally unemancipated call reluctance is closely allied to the separationist pattern. Instead of reluctance to approach friends, there is a barrier to dealing with family members. The same problems—networking, asking for referrals, or asking prospects to simply buy the products they have to offer—keep these would-be heavy hitters from attaining higher levels of productivity.

10. *Telephobics.* Telephobics wish that Alexander Graham Bell had never devised the evil instrument called a telephone. We were all doing fine until it came along to interrupt the workday. Telephobia is a dislike of using the phone to prospect. One-on-one prospecting is no problem, but ask telephobics to get on the phone and they can find a dozen excuses for not wanting to pick it up and make something happen. They don't have trouble calling the country club to reserve a tee-off time, and they don't mind calling a friend to go to lunch, but give them a good lead and a phone, and the emotional short circuit begins to cause tension, stress, and anxiety. This is a learned behavior that can be unlearned through proper diagnosis and procedure. Why would you want to remedy this problem? In this fast-paced, hustle-and-hurry world, the telephone is often the only alternative for reaching good-quality prospects. When you must use it, shouldn't it be as stress-free as possible?

11. *Referral aversives.* Referral aversion is self-explanatory—an aversion to asking virtually anyone to give a name of a prospective client. Hesitating, or completely ignoring this source, has stopped many high-caliber, good-quality sales professionals from garnering top honors and production in this business. A special note here: An MDRT research report has shown clearly that many sales professionals who are currently operating at a mediocre level of success would quickly move up to the next rung of achievement by simply adding "ask for referrals" to the steps in their marketing game plan. Individuals who are highly aversive (meaning they dislike getting referrals or refuse to ask for them) make statements like these: "I haven't earned the right yet." "I feel like I'm begging for business." "It's just too uncomfortable." "The tension is too stressful, so I simply refuse to ask."

How much money is the refusal to ask for referrals costing you? Since you began in the business, how many chances or opportunities have you had to gain a referral and make an easier sale?

The Oppositional Reflex

This evidence of call reluctance has slightly different terminology. The oppositional reflex is a behavior that can cause a significant reduction in income. This type of sales professional begins with defensive argumentation; he or she is always right even when wrong. Constant distractions from prospecting include being very emotional, volatile, angry, or upset. Constant criticism of the company, the managers, and other salespeople is substituted for prospecting and promoting competence, products, and services to prospective buyers. For many people, this emotional lifestyle is the barrier to their achieving top sales performance.

Reflexive habitual criticism is higher in sales managers, trainers, and corporate office support personnel than in the sales professionals they manage and support. The group that has the highest degree of this fault is consultants. If this emotional short circuit can be brought under control, all the energy being lost to it can be directed into the prosperous activities of prospecting. Individuals who cannot control it will never earn what they're worth. If you have this problem, it's costing you thousands of dollars each year.

Which types of call reluctance are blocking you? They are the robbers of your productivity. Call reluctance is not a fear of rejection or a fear of failure. It is your own refusal to make enough contacts and to promote your competence to ready, willing, and able buyers.

Self-Rating Scale

To rate your own personal call reluctance, read each of the following questions and answer as honestly as you can. Indicate Yes or No with a checkmark (√) in the appropriate column.

SELF-RATING SCALE

	Yes	No
1. I probably spend more time planning to promote myself than actually doing it.	___	___
2. I'm probably not trying to promote myself or my products or services as much as I could or should, because I'm not sure it's worth the hassle anymore.	___	___
3. I probably don't try as much as I could or should to initiate contact with influential people in my community who could be prospects for my products or services.	___	___
4. I tend to get uncomfortable when I have to call people on the telephone whom I don't know, and who is not expecting the call, to ask them to do something they may not want to do.	___	___
5. Personally, I think it's demeaning to have to call people whom I don't know, and who are not expecting my call, to promote myself or my products/services.	___	___
6. Personally, self-promotion doesn't really bother me. I just don't apply myself to it very purposefully or consistently.	___	___
7. I would avoid giving a presentation to a group if I could.	___	___
8. Actually, prospecting doesn't really bother me. I could initiate more contacts if I were not involved in so many other activities.	___	___

Self-Rating Scale *(Continued)*

	Yes	No

9. I have clear goals and I like to talk about them; actually, I probably spend more time talking about them than working toward them. ____ ____

10. I seem to need some time to "psych myself up" before I can prospect. ____ ____

11. I tend to spend a lot of time shuffling, planning, prioritizing, and organizing the names on my prospecting list (or cards), before I actually put them to use. ____ ____

12. Making cold calls (calling on people whom I don't know, who are not expecting me, and who may not want to talk with me) would really be difficult for me to do. ____ ____

13. I tend to feel somewhat uneasy when I self-promote. Deep down, I probably think that promoting oneself is not really respectable or proper. ____ ____

14. To me, making sales presentations to my friends is unacceptable because it would look like I was trying to exploit their friendship. ____ ____

15. I often feel like I am intruding on people when I prospect. ____ ____

16. To me, making sales presentations to members of my own family is out of bounds because it might look like I was trying to exploit my own relatives. ____ ____

(Continued)

Self-Rating Scale *(Continued)*

	Yes	No

17. It is very important to me to find innovative,
    alternative ways to prospect and self-promote
    that are more dignified than the methods
    used by other salespeople.   ____ ____

18. I think that, emotionally, prospecting
    probably takes more out of me than out of
    other sales professionals.   ____ ____

19. I would probably do all right one-on-one,
    but I would get pretty nervous if I found
    out that I had to give a sales presentation
    to a large group of people.   ____ ____

20. Highly educated, professional people
    like lawyers and doctors tend to annoy
    me, so I don't try to initiate promotional
    contact with them, even though I
    probably could.   ____ ____

Total "Yes" responses = _____

Now let's interpret the Self-Rating Scale.

Total Yes Responses

1–2   Either you are experiencing no emotional difficulty associated with prospecting (self-promotion) at the present
time, or you are experiencing distress but are hesitant to
reveal how much.

3–4   You are like most other sales professionals. The fear
of self-promotion is present, but only in low, nontoxic

amounts. It may be occasionally annoying, but it is not likely to be serious if it remains at this level. It should be manageable by simply emphasizing the markets and prospecting techniques you are most comfortable with, and avoiding those that are the most tender.

5–6   You could have moderate levels of call reluctance at the present time. One or more forms of the fear of self-promotion are currently limiting your prospecting to a level below your ability. Your prospecting is probably out of sync with your market potential.

7–8   You have a considerable amount of call reluctance at the present time. Your prospecting is probably only a shadow of what it could be or needs to be. But don't despair. Instead, fasten your seat belt and get ready for some serious self-confrontation.

9–20   You may have enough call reluctance to stop a small sales force. Do you make *any* sales calls? Your attitudes toward prospecting suggest that you must be working for a manager who has the patience of a saint, in a company with no performance standards. Or are you a self-employed consultant?

Impostors

Earlier, the word "impostors" was mentioned. Let's discuss how impostors can also rob you of your productivity.

The first impostor is an individual who is lacking the motivational energy needed to make it as a sales professional—to get to work and to stay focused on the activities that earn the maximum income. The calling, the hours of study, and the stress make running your own business a tough daily routine. Sales professionals with low or little motivation will have difficulty earning what they are worth because their energy will give out before the job is done.

Here are seven reasons and remedies for lack of energy:

1. *Improper diet.* Energy comes from burning the fuel your system gains from food. Do your daily menus nourish your body and provide it with sufficient fuel?

2. *Excessive drinking.* Alcohol dulls the mind and lowers the energy level. Maybe you're drinking too much alcohol.

3. *Excessive smoking.* This is a major source of energy loss. A vitamin program is highly recommended—along with fewer smokes per day.

4. *Lack of exercise, or too much exercise.* Some people don't exercise enough; others exercise too much. Check yourself. If you have either problem, get started on a moderate regimen. Walk whenever you can.

5. *Interrupted or insufficient sleep.* Some people fail to get sufficient amounts of sleep. Some people get too much sleep. How much sleep do you get? Try for a steady amount at a uniform time each night.

6. *Stress.* This is the main cause of death among sales professionals—for the persons as well as the careers. Do you have daily stress? Where is it coming from? Is it related to finances, family, or call reluctance?

7. *Long-term health problems.* Many people who have had bypass surgery, cancer, and other serious health problems show a low motivation score.

If you are currently feeling lethargic or you lack sufficient drive and energy, look at this list and see where you might need to adjust how you are generating or losing energy.

Another impostor and robber of productivity is low or unclear goal focus. This leads to unconcentrated effort, and days filled with tedious, mechanistic tasks. There is no interest in prospecting because there is no clear-cut reason to prospect. Your talents and skills give you no reward, so why use them? It's suggested that you immediately sit down and ask yourself, "Why am I doing this? What are the reasons for me to go and begin to prospect?" If you cannot come up with reasons or targets for you to pursue, make some up. Get excited about your business again. You've developed plenty of knowledge over the years. Companies and individuals need your expertise to solve their challenges. Find reasons for prospecting and you will begin to prospect and close more sales.

The next impostor is one that quite a few people struggle with. Research indicates that an average of 60 to 70 percent of sales professionals diffuse their goals so much that they cannot concentrate on their business. Goal diffusion, or too many goals, keeps a person trying to do too much in too little time. These individuals have so many outside activities to think about that their contact-initiation activities will be the very first to suffer. Decide on and prioritize your targets or goals. Develop a plan of action, and begin! Don't wait or hesitate. Begin now. If you think too much about it, months will have gone by—months you can't replace. Decide to take action *now*.

The last impostor is the information impostor—a sales professional who has a legitimate reason for not prospecting: He or she simply doesn't know how. However, some people masquerade as information impostors when in reality they are overpreparers. This is a very tricky distinction. Do you know how to prospect and sell? Do you tell yourself you don't know, when you really do?

This section began with a series of questions. Let's end with a series of statements. Businesses and families need the products and services you offer. Businesses and families need the knowledge, skill, and ability you possess to solve their problems. The companies you represent need your production. You and your family are at their best when you are prospecting and closing sales. As psychologist William James suggested: If you want to honestly do something about your [call reluctance], you must start immediately, start flamboyantly, and make no excuses or exceptions. Now go close more sales!

Five Characteristics of a Strong Closer

1. A strong closer enters every interview expecting to sell the prospect. Money goes to money, and salesmindedness produces sales. It isn't enough to "take part"—the strong closer goes into every interview feeling like a winner.

2. A strong closer makes the purpose of the call clear on the first visit. This sales professional makes no apologies and does not sail under false colors. He or she states the reasons why the prospect should investigate the merit of the intended proposal.

3. A strong closer qualifies the prospect on the very first interview. Can this person buy? Is this person ambitious? Does this person have character? Does this person have a sense of responsibility toward family and company? The sales professional's main job is to separate the prospects from the suspects, and the principal qualification centers around this question: "Do you have long-range obligations and plans that are important to you?" If there are no plans, this person is not a prospect. If long-range plans are not vitally important to a person, he or she should be eliminated from consideration as a prospect. And eliminate anyone who really can't buy. Much of the strong closer's success lies in the ability to

eliminate suspects early and to concentrate selling efforts on prospects who can be sold.

4. A strong closer builds the close from the start of the sales interview. The sole purpose of the interview is to close business and, from the very first words, the strong closer is building up motivation for a favorable decision. By doing this, the strong closer incorporates the interview and the close into one continuous operation.

5. A strong closer is a person of conviction. He or she believes implicitly in what is being sold, and this belief rubs off. This person is not afraid to introduce a motivating story into the close, and employs the proper balance between logic and emotion. The strong closer's convictions, more than his or her words, tell the prospect: "This product is worth a great deal more to you and your family/company than the commission is worth to me."

Closing Techniques

Back in the good old days when Grandmother baked a cake, she would stoke up the kitchen range with fuel, put the cake in the oven, and then let it bake. By a combination of experience, intuition, and watching the clock, plus judicious poking with a broom straw, she knew just when to take the cake out.

Today, cake baking has changed. The recipe book gives a precise formula that includes a specific baking time and an exact temperature. The oven now operates on gas or electricity and has a thermostat with an automatic timer. When the time is up, the buzzer rings and the cake is ready to be removed from the oven.

Many sales professionals would like to have a buzzer ring when their prospects are ready to buy. They look on the close as a mysterious process in which only a master sales professional, through some sixth sense, recognizes the psychological moment to take action. It is true that as sales professionals gain experience in closing, they will develop a keen feel for the prospect's reactions and their timing will improve, but it is doubtful that closing will ever be a process as automatic as baking a cake.

Most prospects just aren't that obvious. Buzzers don't ring. Nor does every sales professional keep the interview at the same oven temperature. Fortunately, however, there is nothing so mysterious or tricky or unique about closing that a capable sales professional needs an alarm to indicate when to begin. The following description illustrates how a sales professional narrows the presentation, step by step, to help the prospect reach the right decision.

Narrowing the Interview

Good closers build their close on the broad base of the total interview. They begin the interview expecting to make a sale. Then, step by step, as the interview progresses, they build up and emphasize reasons for the prospect to buy.

Even the most successful sales professionals have no automatic alarm, and they can't depend wholly on intuition to tell them when to close. Instead, they narrow the interview by imitating what Grandmother used to do. They test with a "broom straw" to find out how near the deal is to being baked.

The broom straw is the trial close: doing or saying something that will show the sales professional what effect has been made on the prospect. It's a "How'm I doing?" device that can tell the sales professional as much about the sale as the straw told Grandmother about her cake. Used often enough and with reasonable skill, broom straws are most effective in narrowing the interview and indicating the direction the close should take.

Here are some broom-straw examples:

"[Prospect's Name], you told me at the start of our visit that purchasing quality products for your company has been a real problem in the past. A product like this would help you solve that problem, wouldn't it?"

With this straw, the sales professional has made a trial close. If the prospect agrees, the interview has been narrowed and the close might be in sight. If the prospect disagrees, hedges, or asks a question, there is more selling to do. The cake needs a little more baking.

"[Prospect's Name], you'd like that feature in this type of product, wouldn't you?" or, "[Prospect's Name], as you see, this product includes all the features you deemed necessary for you to buy it. By owning it, you would have no need to look further for a similar product, would you?"

Broom straws sample the prospect's attitude. They secure commitments that narrow the range of topics to be discussed. They frequently lead directly into the close itself.

It will pay any sales professional to remember (and make a record of) leading questions that are developed and used in interviews. With only slight modifications to fit a specific prospect's situation, they can be used again and again—and they'll be effective because they're the sales professional's own.

In addition to the broom-straw or trial close method of narrowing the interview, other widely used techniques include: (1) implied consent, (2) decision on a minor point, (3) the end-all alternative, (4) start an action, and (5) the takeaway.

Implied Consent

When the implied consent technique is used, it is often unnecessary to ask for a decision. The sales professional merely goes on to complete the sale. When the interview has reached the point where there is reason to believe the prospect considers the plan a logical and desirable answer for the problem that is present, why insist on an admission that this person is ready to buy? Ask people whether they want quality products and services and peace of mind, and their answer is apt to be "Yes." Ask them whether they want to spend more to get it, and they almost have to say "No." This is human nature, so why run the risk of a "No" if it can be avoided? Implied consent makes it easy for a prospect to buy. Don't conduct the sales interview as though you were impaneling a jury. The prospect need not pledge: "I do now solemnly swear that I have made up my mind to buy this product." Implied consent takes for granted that the sale is made. If the prospect does not indicate otherwise, it *is* made.

But what if the prospect does not go along with the sales professional's assumption? Is the interview over? By no means. The sales professional simply continues with the presentation. Nothing has been lost, and the sales professional has gained another opportunity to narrow the area of discussion by asking, "Why?"

Despite the proved success of the implied consent technique, fear prevents its more widespread use—fear that the prospect may say, "Now hold on. I haven't decided what I am going to do about this." What has the sales professional lost? The prospect has resisted on a minor point, but a resourceful sales professional has many more advantages to exhibit.

One of the easiest ways to use implied consent is to start filling out the sales contract agreement. Begin with the questions to which the prospect is least likely to object. "Now, [Prospect's Name], let me get some information from you. What is your home address? How long have you lived there?" If the prospect doesn't halt this, the sales professional has made a sale. If the prospect does, the selling interview continues.

Decision on a Minor Point

The purpose of getting the prospect's decision on a minor point is that it is much easier for a person to make a series of small decisions that add up to one big decision than it is to make the big decision by itself.

Buying products or services is a big decision for most people. Agreeing to the initial interview, selecting a particular product to discuss, and highlighting product benefits are all minor decisions. Break the big sale down into a long series of little sales that are easy to make. Here's how one MDRT sales professional does this:

> If I am going to sell to a farmer, I first sell the idea of getting the farmer down off the tractor for a little visit. Then I sell the farmer on getting in the car to take a break. Then I start talking about saving money, and sell the idea of letting me show how my products can help the farmer. I keep that up all the way.

This approach is typical of most sales. The sales professional who thinks of starting the close as soon as the prospect grants an interview is starting a chain reaction of small decisions that can easily and logically lead to the big decision without once asking the big question.

The End-All Alternative

In offering a so-called end-all alternative, the sales professional is giving the prospect a choice between two minor decisions. Whichever decision the prospect makes closes the sale. Here are some examples:

✓ "[Prospect's Name], would you prefer to make your payments once a year or twice?" (Assumed consent is combined with the offer of a choice between two seemingly minor decisions.)

✓ "Would you prefer to see Dr. Smith or Dr. McMahon?"

✓ "Would you want to make one lump-sum payment, or would you prefer to have it on a definite monthly payment plan?"

Each interview, depending on the prospect, the need, and the nature of the plan, offers many opportunities to employ an alternative close.

Start an Action

"[Prospect's Name]," the sales professional asks while beginning to fill out the paperwork, "how do you spell your middle name?"

An easy question to ask, but it starts an action that the prospect will actually have to stop, if he or she has no intention to buy. Implying consent, getting decisions on minor points, offering alternatives, and then going on to complete the sale might seem to add up to high-pressure tactics, but they're not, unless the person has no real need or honestly cannot afford the product or service. (In this event, no amount of pressure is likely to result in a satisfactory sale.) Where there is a need and the client is able to make the purchase, the closing techniques simply make it easy for prospects to act. There may be only a simple suggestion: "May we take a moment and fill out some basic information on this purchase agreement?" Or, you might summarize the already stated reasons why the prospect should buy: "As I see it, there are only three reasons why you *shouldn't* have this product. The first is that you don't think you need it—and I know that isn't true. The second is that you can't pay for it [maybe you should smile at this point] and we both know *that* isn't true. The third is that you think there is a better product out there—and that's something you can check easily enough." (Then you open a product catalog and compare features of similar products.)

The Takeaway

Fear of loss is a powerful motivating force. People hate to pass up bargains, and sales personnel in all lines have learned to use this fact to advantage in securing prospects' decisions. The Sales professional can urge the prospect to act *now,* before the opportunity to secure a bargain is gone: "[Prospect's Name], on the day after tomorrow, the prices for this product will increase 10 percent because our discount offer will expire. Perhaps, if you are really intending to make this purchase, the time to buy is now."

Realistic Selling

A term that many basketball referees have learned is "realistic officiating." What does realistic officiating mean, and how does it relate to selling? First, here's a basketball example: A player has the ball and is driving, uncontested, toward the basket for a lay-up shot. There is nobody within 30 feet of him. One of the officials, who is in the backcourt, sees a player make physical and relatively hard contact with an opposing player. This occurrence is 60 feet from the player going in for the shot. Should the official blow the whistle and call the foul? The answer is "No." Neither team gained an advantage because of the push. With realistic officiating, you don't take away a good play because of something insignificant.

In selling, you can also be "realistic." You can act in a manner that will best cause the results and goals each individual is looking for. Don't waste your time with items that are insignificant. Use every hour wisely. Do you prepare properly for every interview with a prospect? Or do you leave your office at the last possible moment, set overland speed records on the way to the appointment, run to the prospect's office briskly, and walk into the reception area miraculously transformed into a mild-mannered individual?

We all have the ability to sell, and it's assumed that we all have knowledge of the products. The difference that brings success is preparation—taking the time to sit quietly and contemplate what may or may not occur in the upcoming sales appointments, or reviewing what a prospect asked you to do in advance of an appointment. Is the outcome different from his or her request? Why? Are you prepared for the prospect to say something different from what you want the prospect to say? Remember: Your prospects' thoughts are likely to be completely different from yours.

If you're seeing new prospects, learn, in advance, about them, their businesses, and their business neighbors. In most meetings, a client or prospect will, at some point, put you on the spot; your brain will search frantically for a legitimate answer or response. You've probably been there, so you know that you can generally offer one of three answers: the right answer, the wrong answer, or "I don't know."

Most successful sales professionals feel more comfortable steering away from any reply that seems to be a wrong answer. With good systematic preparation, you should have enough right answers in your brain that, if needed, you should feel extremely comfortable stating "I do not know the answer."

Preparation gives you the wonderful ability to be comfortable with saying, "I don't know." Basketball officials prepare diligently in what they call a "pregame." In a typical pregame session, they go over the rules and essentials of the game. There are two or three officials, so they must work closely and in sync.

Ninety minutes prior to the game, they sit down and go over pregame items such as:

- ✓ What happens when we blow the whistle at the same time?
- ✓ What moves constitute blocking, charging, and basket interference?
- ✓ How will we handle the coaches when they become vocal?

Prepare as much as possible for your interviews. Be prepared for the unexpected because it will surely happen.

Agenda Selling

The agenda has become a favorite tool of many sales professionals. In a typical interview, the agenda is introduced to the prospect very early. This procedure provides a track to run on. It is important to let your prospect know what you are going to talk about.

Here is a typical agenda format. It's simple, concise, and not too detailed:

- ✓ Construction of a daily schedule.
- ✓ The rules.
- ✓ Preparation.
- ✓ Agenda.
- ✓ The interview.
- ✓ Philosophy.

When prospects see an agenda, they know what will be discussed. There are no surprises. They know where the meeting will begin and where it will end. When you use an agenda, you are developing a sense of order and professionalism within your presentation. If prospects inform you that one of the topics on your agenda is not applicable, that's great! You're saved from innocently talking about something that your audience does not want to hear.

At times, a sale will occur prior to the completion of the agenda. This is even better; if appropriate, you can finish your agenda at another meeting. Agenda selling also adds to your style. You may find that longtime clients anticipate your use of an agenda as part of your routine, a common denominator that guides them through each of your presentations. This can only develop a better relationship.

The Interview

Now that we have talked about the rules, the agenda, and your preparation for the appointment, let's discuss the interview itself. Certain things that you can add to your interview will enhance your chances of a better relationship and a sale. An important point: Closing occurs not only because of what you know, but because of how you present your knowledge. In addition to the words you say, your demeanor, your body moves, and how you are positioned in the room can determine whether you close successfully.

During the interview, try to position yourself so that you can see most of a prospect's body: full face and eyes, arms and hands, feet, etc. If the prospect is behind a desk, try to position yourself on the side of the desk, for fuller reciprocal effect. What is occurring here is assisting the prospect in opening up to you. Eye contact over a large desk cluttered with papers, photos, an in/out box, and obstacles such as computers, is detrimental to your presentation. Control your destiny a little more by giving yourself an advantageous position.

You must develop your own personal philosophy and your own realistic selling perspective, while maintaining respect for and awareness of the different philosophies and viewpoints of your clients.

Try to remember that your prospects and/or clients have unique methods of learning, understanding, and appreciating information. No matter what thinking process you use, your prospect does not think in exactly the same manner.

This short quote from John Stuart Mill's 1859 essay, "On Liberty," seems impossible to outgrow:

> If all mankind minus one, were of one opinion, and only one person were of the contrary opinion, mankind would be no more justified in silencing that one person, than he, if he had that power, would be justified in silencing mankind.

Don't force your feelings about what you want prospects to buy. Give prospects or clients direction and a thorough education. It's their decision and their money. Remember, they have already proved to be good decision makers: They have allowed you to talk to them.

Close in Steps

The following observation is that of a MDRT associate who has achieved overwhelming success in his sales career. In this case example, you will see how this sales professional was able to turn a negative sales scenario into a winning presentation.

In the area where I live and work, there is a great deal of construction activity going on. In my daily travel, I noticed that on a number of construction sites there were many concrete trucks painted green. Once I started to look for these trucks, they appeared to be everywhere. I looked in the Yellow Pages of our phone book and found a large ad for this concrete company, which proudly stated that they were established in 1930. Therefore, they could be a family business, and their great number of trucks on the road would indicate they were doing very well.

While driving with a client, whom we shall, for the purpose of discussion, call Mr. Reference, we passed one of these green cement trucks. Mr. Reference is in the building materials business, so I asked him if he knew the people who owned these trucks. His answer was, "Sure. Green Valley Concrete. I know them very well."

Very simply and directly, I asked him if he would telephone them and recommend that they take a look at the type of work that I do. He was happy to do it, and by the end of that day, I was informed by my client that the way was cleared for me to go ahead and call Mr. Green for an appointment.

When I phoned Mr. Green, I said that Mr. Reference had asked me to call him because he felt that Green Valley Concrete could profit from our services in the same way that he had. Mr. Green replied, "Yes, he mentioned that, but really, all of our financial concerns are pretty well taken care of. We recapitalized the corporation recently. We all have wills, and we bought as much life insurance as we are going to buy, about two years ago. And moreover, we probably couldn't qualify for any more even if we did want it."

Well, with those strong words of encouragement, I took a deep breath and said, "The things you have done, Mr. Green, show me that you are the type of individual who cares enough to do everything possible to attend to his business and estate affairs. That's exactly why I think you might want to see the idea that saved Mr. Reference over $1 million."

After a brief moment of silence, I heard a short "OK" on the other end of the phone. I asked him if I could see him on Tuesday morning at 9:00 A.M. He agreed. And then I commented that, since we have all of the backup material for the meeting in our office, he would get more out of it if we met here.

Tuesday morning came around, and I went through my usual preinterview mental preparation. This involves sitting back, closing my eyes, reflecting on the person about to come into my office, and thinking to myself that the most important thing I can do today is motivate this man to want to do business with me.

Once having finished this, despite its usefulness, I was still a little edgy waiting for Mr. Green. Thoughts even flashed through my mind about what a relief it would be if he didn't show up at all. Well, my weakhearted wish came true! He didn't show up! After waiting half an hour, I called him and discovered that he thought we were meeting in his office and had been sitting there wondering what kind of an irresponsible person I was! We rescheduled for after lunch, in his office, and finally, there we were, face-to-face.

He was behind his desk in a defensive posture. The first thing I did was to eliminate this walnut barrier by asking him if I could slide my chair around to the side so that we might look at some ideas together. This put us on the same team, in a position to review the type of work that I do and how it could help him. We were together analyzing his problems. I wasn't selling anything. I was helping him buy.

Our first job was to review what other wealthy people in his position have gone through. We looked first at an attorney who died without a will and lost 50 percent of his estate—half the product of his life's work. This prompted Mr. Green to comment that his father had died four years earlier, and, because of a lack of planning, they were still paying his estate taxes on a 15-year stretchout with the government, with interest on this loan as high as 20 percent. When he said that, I knew we could help *him! Once I had established other people's difficulty in handling the problems caused by death, and, in this particular case, obtained a confession from Mr. Green that he had suffered from a lack of planning himself, the case I was making for the value of my services was well under way.*

We next looked at an example of the work I was offering to do for him. This involved a complete analysis of his and the other family members' current personal and corporate plans and goals. I finished by showing him a list of other clients, many of whom he knew of or knew personally. Then I looked him squarely in the eye and asked him if this service could be of value to him. He said, "Yes, it could."

Now let's analyze what I just sold to Mr. Green. The first thing he bought was confidence in me. The second thing he bought was the value of my services. And that's all he bought that day. There was no sale—not even a remote attempt to sell my products and services. I asked him simply for a gentlemen's agreement and said this: "If we do this work and if it indicates the need for one of our products, and if you agree that this is the best solution to your problem, then we would expect that you buy from us. Is that fair enough?" Mr. Green's answer: "Sure, that's fair enough."

I then told him what was needed to get started: personal and corporate financial statements, personal and corporate income tax returns, insurance policies, wills, trusts, and all other pertinent documents. In short, everything. After collecting these items, I scheduled a follow-up appointment to review any details about which I had questions.

For me, the follow-up is a critical point in this entire process; it is where the prospect becomes a client without even buying anything yet. In this case, it worked like this: I said to Mr. Green, "This completes all of the personal and financial information we need to do a quality job for you. The final thing we need to do is to schedule a medical exam—at no cost to yourself, of course. This medical exam will give us a totally accurate and complete picture of your present situation. In other words, when we come back to you with our recommendations, if there is a need for life insurance, you will know exactly what is available to you and at what price, so that you can make a decision knowing that you have all of the vital facts."

Mr. Green looked up at me and said, "Well, why don't you just assume that I'm healthy and base any figures you want to show me on that?" My response was, "I'm sorry, Mr. Green, but it's impossible to do a first-class job for you that way. You see, you can't afford to have us make assumptions about anything. We won't be assuming anything about your financial arrangements or your objectives. Your plan has to be constructed on the facts and based upon current tax law; otherwise it's useless. You don't have any objection to going to the doctor, do you, Mr. Green?" He tentatively replied, "No, I guess not." Here, a giant step was made. His "No" was actually a "Yes" in my ears. And my experience has been that, in almost every case, the entire sale is made with that one word—"No."

As you have seen, despite Mr. Green's periodic objections and reluctance, he vitally needs somebody like you or me to motivate him to do what, in his heart, he knows he must do. He did not agree to the physical exam solely as a result of my logic, sound as it was. He ultimately agreed to it because, deep in his heart, he already suspected his present insurance was inadequate and that he should and must prepare himself to acquire more.

The basic facts in this case are not uncommon for this marketplace. Mr. Green and his brother own Green Valley Concrete together. Their father started the company in 1930; they inherited it from him, and they wanted to make sure the company remains in the bloodline of the Green family at their deaths. In addition to the company, they each have invested heavily in *investment real estate. The Green family doesn't like govern-ment interference, they don't like taxes; and they are not partic-ularly fond of life insurance either.*

The results of Mr. Green's physical exams were perfect, and sitting on my desk were four insurance policies in the amount of $1 million each. Now let me tell you how the case actually progressed.

As we discussed, there were two segments to this sale. The first was to insure the brothers for the buy/sell funding, and the second was to insure the wives for the growing estate tax liability.

My sales presentations are prepared and built around at-tempting to make the sale with a bare minimum of objections. My closing ratio goes way down if the prospect and I end up doing battle in the Roman Coliseum. To avoid this type of con-frontation in the Green case, I tried to think of every possible objection they could have beforehand, and then answer those objections in my presentation, without Mr. Green ever having to raise them. By answering objections before they were raised, Mr. Green would not be compelled to build his own case against my suggestions and then be forced to back down if I were to prevail.

I knew Mr. Green would probably object to buying any more insurance to fund the buy/sell agreement. He might feel that they could just handle a buy-out from earnings at the time of death, rather than "spend" money on insurance premiums today. I pre-pared a one-page illustration which showed the effect a redemp-tion for $1 million would have if carried out with no life insurance over a 10-year period at 10 percent interest. The corpo-rate outlay, paid to Mr. Green's sister-in-law, would be over $13,000 per month for this $1 million debt. At the end of 10 years, the total outlay would far exceed the original $1 million.

Next, we looked at the advantage of using life insurance for the redemption funding. I explained to Mr. Green that by buying life insurance, the corporation could have a tax-free credit to its surplus account in exchange for each premium it paid. This tax-free increase would exceed the premiums in each year after year two.

"Therefore," I said, "by using life insurance, you will be increasing the company's surplus account on a tax-free basis. At the same time, you will be guaranteeing that even if your brother dies tonight, you won't be forced to sign checks made out to your sister-in-law for over $13,000 per month for the next 10 years."

After saying this, I could see by Mr. Green's entire body language that his objections had been defused and that he had accepted this logic. With this implied consent, I moved on to the second phase of the presentation, which was more difficult. My job was to motivate Mr. Green to provide for a need he did not yet have. I anticipated that the primary objection to be dealt with here was the feeling that he would just worry about it later, when the problem really came into being.

My strategy developed along these lines. We had a conversation about the past. I asked him, if he could go back and change the planning they had done with his father's estate (let's say, 10 years ago) and they had the opportunity to insure him, would that have been a smart idea? He said, "In hindsight, of course it would." (As you will recall, they were still paying the estate taxes on his father's estate.)

I then said, "It strikes me that is exactly the position you are in today with your own family. From what you have shown me you are doing, you and your brother are programmed for growth. Is it fair to say that within the next 5 to 10 years the value of your estate will double?" He told me it was a fair estimate. I said, "You've got what may be a once-in-a-lifetime opportunity here. By setting up a guaranteed source of tax-free cash today, for tomorrow's needs, you will have time on your side. What I mean by *that is, if we look at insuring Mrs. Green today, for the taxes that will be due tomorrow, you can discount your premiums more than you will ever be able to again. Mrs. Green will never be any younger, and she will never be any healthier than she is today. Let's take a look at how you can use deductible corporate dollars to provide this totally tax-free cash the moment it is needed."*

We then examined the illustration, which works as follows. The corporation would bonus Mr. Green the money for the premium and therefore deduct it. In the corporation's high tax bracket, this means that the government will now be paying one-half of the premium with tax savings. Since Mr. Green is in a very low tax bracket, his out-of-pocket cost will be less than what term insurance would cost. A further tax saving is then achieved by gifting the premium to a "Super-Trust" and removing this asset from estate taxation. Again, the government, in effect, is paying half of the cost through savings in estate taxes.

I finished my explanation of the tax savings available and asked Mr. Green, "Isn't it amazing how little the insurance can cost when you set up in this way, with the government paying for more than half of it?" He said he had never seen anything like it. After a lingering silence, I softly said, "Can you think of any reasons why we shouldn't go ahead with this?" His reply, once again, was the magic word, "No."

Within five minutes I was out the door with a check in hand, and Mr. Green is now a satisfied client who will refer us to the next family business in need of our help.

Chapter 3

Closing Techniques

There is more than one way to close, as the best salespeople know. In fact, there are many ways. Which closing method is best—implied consent, third-party story, series of agreements, impending change, and so on—depends on the prospect, the situation, and the sales professional's style.

Close the Case Before It Opens: Twelve Techniques

You are probably well aware that being a sales professional offers you many avenues of success. But these avenues do have their bumps and sharp turns; nothing is straightforward and easy. The following observation of a very successful MDRT sales associate is a case in point. One day, a peer approached him and said, "How do you find the sales business so easy?" The associate was quick to remind him that, although he was doing well, there was nothing about sales that he found easy. "I would like share with you," he said, "that even though it appears easy to an outsider, it isn't to me. The secret is a proper attitude."

When you look at sales techniques, there are really six methods that can be used to make the sale: (1) prospecting, (2) phoning, (3) interviewing, (4) proposing, (5) closing, and (6) referrals. MDRT sales professionals emphasize the importance of closing, and how good closing techniques will lead to excellent prospecting, phoning, interviewing, and referrals.

You've probably heard this countless times: Enthusiasm is the number-one ingredient to closing success. At least 50 percent of all closing effectiveness comes from your enthusiasm—your excitement about the product. As a matter of fact, one of the best definitions of a sale is: A sale takes place when there is a *transfer* of enthusiasm. In other words, when you transfer your enthusiasm about your products and services into the mind of your prospects, a sale takes place. Of course, this requires that you have some enthusiasm to transfer into the mind of the other person.

The most effective sales professionals know their products, believe in their products, have confidence in their products, love their products, and believe their products have very worthwhile benefits for their clients. If you don't believe in your products, if you don't love your products, if you wouldn't use them yourself, if you wouldn't sell them to your mother or your best friend, then you probably won't close the sale. You have to transfer your enthusiasm into the mind of prospects to cause them to buy.

With regard to enthusiasm, it isn't the rah-rah, jump-around type of enthusiasm; what is meant is called *constrained* enthusiasm. The enthusiasm is kept inside you like a boiling kettle with a lid put on it, so that you literally whistle with enthusiasm. You project a sort of dynamic tension or excitement, but it isn't in the speed of your speech or in your actions; it is contained within. Constrained enthusiasm has perhaps one of the most powerful effects on human personality that you can imagine. As Ralph Waldo Emerson said, "Nothing great was ever accomplished without enthusiasm."

The second psychological quality is confident expectation. You must confidently expect that the person is going to say "Yes" if you ask often enough. You should truly believe that every person you see wants to do business with you. Why not? You have a great product and provide great service! If you ask prospects to buy, you must confidently expect them to buy. So act expectantly. If at first you *do* succeed, try to hide your astonishment. The more confidently you expect to sell, the more likely it is that you will sell. Again, confidence in selling comes from knowledge, from practice, from experience, and from believing that the product will do what you say it can do.

In the process of selling, there are other steps that you have to take. The first step is qualifying. You cannot sell a product until you have thoroughly qualified the prospect. Many people have had this experience: They walked into a store or onto a used-car lot, and someone came up and said, "Why don't you take it?" or "Are you going to buy it today?" The salesperson tried to sell something without even asking what the customer wanted or needed. Nothing makes you more furious than having someone try to sell to you without determining your needs. Qualify prospects by asking yourself these four questions:

1. Does the prospect need what I'm selling?
2. Can the prospect use what I'm selling?
3. Can the prospect afford the product?
4. Does the prospect want the product?

Before you can close, prospects have to demonstrate that they have a desire for the benefits of the product or service that you can provide. Only after you have gone through the presentation, qualified the prospect with a "Yes" to all four questions, and confirmed that the prospect *wants to buy* what you're selling, are you in a position to begin closing.

Most closes happen during the presentation. Actually, the close begins before you even present your information. The first phase of a close is on the telephone. Good phone technique will cause the sale to be "closed before it is opened." The key reason why the closing technique is important is because the moment of closing is always difficult; it is always a moment of tension. You might call this "buyer's remorse in advance." Whenever prospects reach the point when they have to make an important decision—put out money, or lay themselves on the line with a key decision—tension builds inside them. This tension is called the fear of failure, and every human being has it.

For the customer, the tension in the closing moments of the sale is caused by the fear of making a mistake, the fear of buying the wrong product, the fear of paying too much, and the fear of being criticized by other people. What happens when people have this fear? They back away, and they say things like, "Um, let me think it over, leave me some material," or " Could you call me back next week; I have to talk it over with someone else," or "I have to check it out, I can't afford it"—and so on. These are simply the prospects' ways of telling you, "If I make this decision, it may not be the right thing for me."

Sales professionals all have a fear that the prospect will say "No"—the fear of being rejected. To conquer it, they try to structure their lives not to hear "No." If you have uneasiness about people saying "No" to you, you picked a very tough profession. You must be aware that some people are going to say "No," and one of the key factors for success in sales is being prepared to hear that. Every "No" that you hear brings you closer to a "Yes." If a prospect says, "No, I don't think so," you must learn to just let it roll off your back. You even have to pretend that the "No" wasn't said. You must regard the first "No" as a phony rejection and find out why the prospect said "No." You must also realize that a "No" is not personal.

If a prospect says "No," to you, he or she is not rejecting you as a person. In most cases, the prospect is saying "No" to a whole package of reasons. When you reach the end of the sales presentation, you have done your prospecting, you have covered all facets of your presentation, and you have overcome some rejections. Now you come to the final moment. You know that the prospect wants to buy, but there is an inner voice encouraging "sales resistance." There is fear and uneasiness. Tension starts to build up, and your job is to get through this tense moment as rapidly and as painlessly as possible.

Closing techniques are not techniques for manipulating people; they are not techniques to get people to buy things they don't want and don't need, can't use and can't afford. They are techniques to get people past that moment of tension. A professional closer takes the person smoothly past the point of close; an unprofessional closer may say, at the end of the presentation, "Well, what do you think?" Can you predict what the prospect will reply, as his or her tension starts to build up? The prospect says, "Well, I think I'll think it over; I think I have to talk it over with someone else." Even if the prospect wants the product, the tension wins.

Described here are 12 closing techniques that work for MDRT sales professionals. They can work for you, helping you to "close the case before it is opened."

1. Getting the appointment.

Do you routinely use the telephone to get appointments? Almost all sales professionals do! Do you notice how difficult and frustrating it is? Of course you do! Many sales professionals refrain from using the telephone because they have been turned down so many times on the telephone that the very thought of it causes them to be frustrated and tense. Instead, they find every other possible way to make contact. But the telephone is still the finest and the fastest way. If you know how to use it properly in approaching a prospect, the key to success is simple.

The first thing you say to the prospect should be something that grabs attention and points to the result or benefit of the product. How many of you, when calling someone you don't know, say: "This is so and so calling, and I'm calling [because of whatever reason]," or maybe you actually say, "to discuss [the product you are selling]"? This is ordinary and typical. When you call someone, always use the prospect's full name; this approach exudes confidence. For example, "[Prospect's Name], I'm calling with a way for you to significantly increase the value of your business." You now have your prospect's immediate attention. One thing is sure: The prospect doesn't care about *your* name until later in this phone conversation.

When you introduce yourself, you can say, "My name is [Your Name]; last name is spelled [then spell the name out]." This strategy allows your name to be reinforced. One popular line among MDRT associates is: "I'm calling with a way you can make and save money at the same time." The prospect doesn't know who you are yet, but he or she is going to want to talk with you.

Once again, remember that positive attitude and excitement are everything. Never discuss anything negative. If people say that it is raining out, you can say, "That's OK, it is not snowing."

An MDRT associate, when cold calling, found he could get appointments seven out of ten times with qualified prospects, using the following very simple technique:

I would call and ask the secretary, "Who is the person who makes decisions in this area—who is the person who makes the decisions about your business?" The secretary would say, "That would be Mr. Smith." I would say, "Fine. What is his first name, please?" "Bill Smith." I would then ask to speak to Mr. Smith. "Hello, Bill. How would you like to see a method that would increase benefits and reduce costs by 10 to 30 percent over the next 12 months?" Now, if you are speaking to the right person, the question will be aimed at something that is relevant and something that the other person needs. Do you know any person or corporation that would not want to save significant dollars?

At that point, you go into the close. When you are telephoning for an appointment, you are telephoning to sell an appointment, not to sell a product. The biggest mistake sales professionals make is to start describing their products on the telephone. The person then says, "No, I am sorry; I am not interested, can't afford it, don't have the time," and so on. So all you do is sell the prospect 10 minutes. You say, "That's exactly what I want to talk to you about. I need 10 minutes of your time. I will show you what I've got and you can judge for yourself if it is what you want." The person may ask something like, "How much is it?" They don't even know what "it" is. You say, "[Prospect's Name], if it is not exactly what you are looking for, there is no charge at all." This is a very good response. This gets the price out of the way. Then the person says, "Can you tell me a little bit about it?" You can say, "Well, that's why I need just 10 minutes of your time; just 10 minutes, and I will be able to show you the benefits of my product, and you can judge for yourself."

Remember this: Good prospects are hard to find, are always busy, and are hard to reach. Poor prospects are not busy and they are easy to reach. If you call somebody to ask for an appointment and the reply is, "Sure, come on over anytime," you can be sure the person isn't going to buy anything from you. Be very sharp when you use the telephone. If the person says, "Could you send me something in the mail?" you can say, "I would like to send it to you in the mail, but you know how bad the mail is. Why don't I drop it off personally sometime this afternoon?" If the prospect is at all serious, he or she will say, "Okay, drop it off personally this afternoon." And you respond, "Okay, I'll be in your neighborhood about 3 o'clock. I'll drop it off personally." Don't mail the information. When people say, "Send me some information in the mail," what they are saying is, "Go away, I'm not interested." And when you send it to them in the mail, it goes right from the secretary into the wastebasket.

Don't ask for 30 minutes, because you might have to wait for weeks or perhaps forever. If you ask for 10 minutes, you can always be slipped in. Be very flexible in establishing the time. Typically, you might hear, "Call me on Monday and we'll set up an appointment." You should say to the prospect, "I've got my calendar right here; is your calendar handy?" Dumb question, of course, the prospect is at his or her desk, and the calendar *is* handy. You say, "Let's set up a time right now. How about 10 o'clock Monday morning?" Don't allow yourself to be put off by having to call back on Monday. That's just another way of the prospect's avoiding you. The very best customers you'll ever have are the ones you have to fight to see. So just be persistent and firm. "Nothing great was ever done without much enduring." If you cannot close on a telephone appointment, you cannot get to first base.

2. The demonstration close.

This close is extremely effective because you are getting a commitment before you ever begin. Once again, "Close before the case is opened." The demonstration close is what you do (1) to qualify the prospect in the opening statement and (2) to get a clear statement that the prospect is in a position to buy and pay for this product.

"If I could show you an excellent product, Mr. Smith, are you in a position to put $5,000 into it right now?" The prospect says, "Well, I don't know. No, I haven't got $5,000." You say, "How about $4,000?" "Well, I don't know." "How about $3,000?" "Well, yes, $3,000." "If I could show you the best product you have ever seen, you would put $3,000 into it?" "Well, yes, if you could show me." What you have done is changed the focus of discussion. You're not discussing whether the person will listen to your presentation. The discussion topic is whether you can demonstrate that you actually have a product that is as good as that. You are asking whether this person is in a position to make a decision right now. The prospect will say, "Yes." Now, after you go through your presentation, the person can't say, "Well, I have to check with the boss," or "I have to speak to my friend Stanley." The prospect has already said, "Yes, I have the money; yes, I am qualified; yes, I am in a position to make a decision." This is a good strong opening question that grabs attention. It works for almost any sale situation.

3. The decision close.

You use this right at the beginning of the sales presentation. The purpose of the decision close is to get the person to commit to give a decision at the end of the presentation, instead of saying, "I have to think it over." You simply say, "[Prospect's Name], I am not going to try to sell you anything now. Just relax." He or she says, "Okay, that's good." You say, "All I am going to do is show you some of the reasons why people have bought this product and continue to buy it over the years; and all I ask you to do is look at these reasons, judge for yourself, and tell me one way or the other whether this applies to you and to your situation. Is that fair?" The person will say, "Okay." You have offered a deal: You won't try to sell the product if he or she listens with an open mind to your presentation. At the end of the presentation, the prospect cannot say, "Well, I have to think it over." You say, "[Prospect's Name], you promised you would give me an answer one way or another. It is a very simple quote, you promised you would give me an answer one way or another, and from what you have said, it seems that this product is just ideal for your situation." You can go right through to the close. Positive presenting is always a key to any closing method.

4. The sizzle close.

This close is the most important and the most powerful close of all. Most purchases align with the fact that 90 percent of the buying decisions are based on 10 percent of the product features. In other words, it is up to you to find the one or two things in your presentation that are key selling points to the prospect who is buying the product. Keep mentioning these items over and over again because every time you mention them, the prospect's desire to own your wonderful product increases. Every time you talk about something that is not really important to the prospect, the desire to own this product diminishes. Good sales professionals are people who question skillfully and listen carefully. If you talk to prospects long enough and give them enough chance to talk, they will tell you everything you need to know to sell them. You are only really selling when you are asking questions and people are given the opportunity to tell you what they are looking for—what they want, need, and are concerned about. The more you listen, the sooner you will find out exactly what your prospect wants. Until the product's sizzle—a key benefit—is found, the prospect won't make the buying decision. It is important to make the prospect see the key benefit, the product's sizzle. When people are telling you what they want, listen hard.

5. The "constant check" close.

In this close, you check how far along you are. When you possess the part of the product that the prospect is looking for, you know it is time to begin the close. "Is this what you had in mind?" "Is this an improvement on what you're doing right now?" These are check closes. The wonderful thing about a check is that the prospect can answer "Yes" or "No" and it doesn't end the presentation. If you say, "Is this what you feel good about?" and the prospect says, "No," you say, "Fine, let's look at something else." Or if you say, "Is this the type of product benefit you are looking for?" and the prospect says, "Yes," you win. Good sales professionals rely on check closes throughout, to see how they are doing. They never present a new piece of information without the check close. Once the prospect says "Yes" to the point you mention, move to the next important point or to the close.

For instance, if you were selling a house to a prospect, you would drive up in front of the house and say, "Do you like the outside look of that house, yes or no?" You would then take the prospect inside and say, "Do you like the entry hallway, yes or no?" You would keep asking questions, and the answers would give you feedback that enables you to build a confident picture of exactly what the prospect wants—a tremendous help in closing the sale.

6. The "change places" close.

This close is very simple. You are giving a presentation, and the prospect will not tell you what is his or her "key issue." Remember that in every sales presentation, a key benefit causes prospects to buy, and a key objection keeps them from buying. Until you can find out what the key objection is, and handle it, prospects will never buy from you. Many closing techniques are actually ways of getting a person to tell you what is blocking a buying decision. You say, "[Prospect's Name], would you change places with me just for a second? Put yourself in my shoes. Imagine you are talking to somebody whom you respect, and you are showing that person an idea that is really good for future use, and that person won't tell you why it is not of interest. What questions would you ask, or what feature do you think should be included in this presentation?" This prospect will now tell you what is needed to close the sale.

7. The price close.

Many people say that everybody buys based on price. Have you heard that before—that everybody wants the lowest price? In almost every case, the price is not the major determinant in selling anything. Price is only important when comparing apples with apples. When somebody wants what you have, price is not important. Whenever there is any differentiation in product, price is not the major factor. Your rule should be to never compare apples with apples. Price is a problem because sales professionals make an issue of price. If the prospect says, "How much is it?" and you immediately get into a wrestling match and say it is X number of dollars, the prospect says, "I can't afford that." If you get into an argument, you can never win on price. The basic rule on price is: Price should never come up until the end of a sales presentation, when prospects must give you some money (a deposit or a down payment) or there can be no close. How should you deal with price? When prospects say, "How much is it?" before you have had a chance to tell them what they are getting, simply ask whether price is their only concern. They will probably say, "No." Everything always costs more than prospects expect to pay. Their willingness and their ability to pay are two different things. Nobody is willing, but most people are able. You say, "Let's talk about that a little bit later." If you start a good sales presentation, they are going to get interested. When they say, "How much is this?" you answer: "[Prospect's Name], that's the best part. Can I come to that in a couple of minutes?" The prospect says, "Sure," and you continue the presentation. Try not to get into price, and *never argue* over price. By the time you get to the end of the presentation, you should have spoken so much about the value of what they are going to purchase that when you mention the price, it becomes secondary.

8. *The sudden-death close.*

This is also called the ultimatum close. You have probably had this experience: You make a presentation to a prospect. You allow time for "looking it over." You go back four or five times but hear "We have to think about it a little more." You realize that you are spending too much time going back to the prospect, who still has not made a decision. So you use a sudden-death close. It works at least 50 percent of the time. Whatever business you lose with this close, you would not have had anyway. Besides, you free up time that will allow you to accomplish other closes. Fill out the paperwork for the sale, exactly the way you have discussed it until now, except for the signature. Go back to the prospect and say, "[Prospect's Name], you know we have discussed this quite a bit, and I know this is taking up a lot of your time. Either this is a good idea for you or not. Let's make a decision right now." Then take the paperwork, put it across the desk, put the pen on top of it, and say, "If you will authorize this now, we can get started right away." Then, stay perfectly silent. At the end of every closing technique, the key is to be perfectly silent and wait. Sometimes the silence can get longer and longer, but the longer you wait in absolute silence, the more likely the person will make the buying decision. The only sales pressure you should use in a sales presentation is the pressure of the silence after you have asked the closing question. The basic rule is: He (or She) who speaks first after the closing question loses. Remember, the best time to close the sale is at the end of your presentation, not the next day, or next week. At the end of the sales presentation, the prospect has more fresh information and is closer to making a decision than at any other time.

9. *The fatal alternative close.*

In this popular technique, you close on a minor point. You are giving a sales presentation on a particular product, and you ask,

"Do you want to pay over a long-term period or a short-term period?" It doesn't matter to you whether they pay either way; once they answer, the decision to buy the product has been made. When you are discussing how they wish to pay, you ask, "Would you like to make the payment on the first or the fifteenth?" If they say, "The fifteenth," they have made the decision to buy the product. In other words, you close on a minor question. You do this because it is much easier for the prospect to say, "Well, the fifteenth," than "Yes" or "No" to buying what you're selling. You are a winner no matter what choice is made. Never offer prospects a choice between something and nothing, always make the choices something or something—Product A or Product B. Which house do you like better, contemporary or traditional? Which car do you prefer, the two-door or the four-door? Which type of tires do you want, radial or regular? Always give a choice between two options. You then have an opportunity to continue selling. Don't ever say, "Do you want this or not?" Always say, "Which do you prefer?" This is alternately called "the preference close." Asking people which they prefer is a very good way to find out where you are in the sales presentation. Assuming consent can be an extremely powerful strategy.

10. The Ben Franklin close.

The Ben Franklin close gets good results because it explores how prospects think when they face a decision: they weigh the pros and cons—the reasons for and against making the decision. This is called the Ben Franklin close because he was America's first self-made millionaire. He used to make decisions by taking a piece of paper and drawing a line down the center. He would write all the reasons in favor of making the decision on one side of the paper, and all the reasons opposed to it on the other side. Then he would study the reasons and make a decision. Whenever you start anything complex, Franklin's method is fine for a person who has difficulty making up his or her mind because of a variety of different factors. You say, "[Prospect's Name], let's use the Ben Franklin decision-making method. It is a very simple method. Ben Franklin made decisions on this basis, and he became one of the richest men in America. This is what we will do: Take a piece of paper, draw a line down the center, and let's write all the reasons in favor of making this purchase decision." You restate all the good reasons for buying the product. Then you say, "Is that everything? Can you think of anything else?" When the prospect says, "No, I think this is everything," say, "Okay, now you fill out the other side." Give the prospect the pad of paper and the pen, and sit quietly. The prospect writes one item, maybe two. You then say, "[Prospect's Name], it looks like you have made your decision. When is a good time for delivery of the product?" Now you have assumed consent. Try it; you'll like it. You have nothing to lose; see what happens. Summarize all the reasons for buying the product or service (listed in the order that you want). At the end of that summary, the individual will be at his or her highest buying temperature. Take out the paperwork and start to complete it. If you write the date on it and the prospect doesn't stop you, ask for the exact spelling of the prospect's last name. If the prospect gives you the exact spelling, the prospect has made the decision to buy. If someone says, " I don't want this," be direct and ask, "Why do you feel that way?" The prospect is probably objecting without really knowing why.

11. The relevant story close.

Relevant stories are an effective close because prospects want to know that others have bought what they are considering buying. They want to hear the benefits. Prospects will remember a story about a product or service for years, whereas they'll forget all the technical details in ten minutes. When a prospect is having difficulty, even in the middle of a presentation, tell a relevant story about somebody who hesitated to buy this product and who experienced some loss from that decision. Try to use examples that will shake people up. Explain that, if they go with the contract, they still have ten days, free, to examine it, so they really have nothing to lose. More than statistics, facts, or interest rates, this kind of story causes people to make final decisions.

12. The "please forgive me" close.

Use this close when you've made your presentation, giving it your best shot, and the prospect has resisted but is not giving you a major objection. The prospect doesn't want to give you any ammunition. He or she is just sitting there while you're doing everything possible. You get one excuse after another. The prospect says, "No, well, I don't think so; I'm going to talk it over; I'm not in the market; I don't think we can afford it," and the prospect won't tell you what is really stopping the consent. You know the prospect has the money, and you want the prospect to purchase your product. Finally, you say, "[Prospect's Name], I know you're busy and I thank you very much for your time. I won't take up any more of your day. I'll get going now." You close your briefcase, you get up, and you go to the door. As you get to the door, you put your hand on the doorknob. The prospect immediately begins deciding what task to tackle as soon as you leave. His or her sales resistance drops as soon as you put your hand on the door. You start to open the door, then you turn around and say, "By the way, just before I go, I know you're not going to buy my product today, but I was wondering if you can help me with my presentation. Could you tell me the reason why you are not going with me on this today?" The prospect will tell you the reason and you take your hand off the doorknob. You come back in and set down your briefcase. You say, "I'm so glad you told me, because that is my fault. Obviously, I didn't explain that part of my presentation properly. May I go over it just one more time?" Now you have the key reason to sit down and stay. If you can answer this objection effectively, you should be able to close the majority of the time.

After any of these closes, don't forget referrals. The most important closes you will ever make are those that take you into others. The basic rule is: Never leave a prospect or a purchaser without at least three referrals. Don't ask: "Do you know of anybody who needs my products and services?" Ask prospects to do you a favor. "Promise me that the next time you need what I have to offer, you will call me. Also, if any friends or relatives you know need my products or services, you will think of me. Would you do that for me? Do you promise?" Wait for an answer!

They say, "Well, sure, we'd be pleased to."

"Just one more thing, promise me if you hear of anybody else who wants to consider what I am offering, you will give me a chance to talk to them first. Would you do that for me?"

They say, "Sure, why not," and they shake hands on it. What they don't realize is when a person makes a promise, it locks into the subconscious. By nature, we have a conscience that will not allow us to break promises. One year, two years, three years later, somebody says, "I know somebody who can handle that for you" and you get a call.

Here is another way to get referrals. You finish speaking to the prospect, and you see that nothing will be purchased from you today. You say, "I know you are not in a position to make a decision today, but could you give me the names of two or three people who you think may be able to take advantage of my knowledge and experience?" This is another alternative close ("two or three people"). Most prospects give two names because it's easier, and they will be the first names that come to mind. Tell the prospect that you want people whose success is equivalent to the prospect—family, people they know well, or equals in work responsibility. You say, "Would you happen to have their phone numbers?" Yes, the prospect happens to have their phone numbers, so the phone numbers are retrieved. You've closed on the phone numbers. Then you say, "Which of these prospects should I call first—Stanley or Bill?" Another alternative close. Unless you sense that you're pushing your luck too far, ask the prospect, "Could you call Stanley right now and tell him I'm coming over?" Most prospects will pick up the phone and dial Stanley or whoever else has been named. You can take the introduction from there.

Ask people politely or even order them around good naturedly, and most will do almost anything you suggest. Tell them that their referrals will allow you to service them better. A referral is much more powerful than a cold call because a referral carries the credibility of the person who refers you. With a cold call, you go in with no credibility, so you face a very long sales process. If you have to get to 100 percent credibility before the prospect will buy, a referral gives you a 90 percent head start. If a person whom you know and respect sent someone to see you, wouldn't you listen? Always ask for referrals, and never leave a presentation without three, or at least two, referrals.

Go back to all of the previous customers in your files. Call to ask them how they're doing. Are they happy with the products they have purchased? Do they have any problems or questions? Is there anything you can do for them? If possible, go and see them. Any person who has been in selling for more than 90 days should be working off referrals almost 50 percent of the time. Anyone who is selling longer than one year should be working off referrals 100 percent of the time. Says one MDRT sales professional:

> I get one referral from every person sold and they don't even know it. Every person sold has a doctor. I call every client's doctor. When I call, obviously I get the secretary or nurse. I

always ask for the doctor by his or her first name. This is essential, because it lowers the secretary's resistance. She thinks you are a friend. Everybody always asks for "Dr. So-and so." When the doctor gets on the phone, explain that your client suggested that you call him or her because of recent work you did with the client. It works, and I'm amazed after I tell people this guaranteed method of referrals, that few people actually take advantage of it. I strive to be associated with people for constant referrals.

Every sales professional should be constantly looking for sources of steady business. Keep in mind that selling is easy. Choosing whom to sell to is the difficult part of your business. When you use the above suggestions, remember that closing techniques are sales tools that can be practiced and experimented with. The more tools you have within your sales toolbox, the more likely you are to make a sale. The more products you use from your product line, the more money you make. For some cases, you will need only two or three closing techniques; for others, you'll use all of them. The more you know, the more opportunities you have to close. Here is a piece of advice that has helped many sales professionals dramatically when they were starting their careers: When you are presenting for people who are not going to buy anything, and you know you have nothing to lose, throw the whole book at them. Throw in every closing technique and every objection technique that you can find. Remember, you only really learn sales techniques by being in the arena with a live prospect.

It's worth a fortune to you if your presentation succeeds, so just sit there and keep going until you really, literally, are thrown out. You will learn about how to close good prospects faster than you can possibly imagine. For sales success, act confidently and close openly. A sales close in which you say, "Which do you prefer?" is far more powerful than "Well, why don't you take it!" Say it confidently, as though you *expect* the other person to buy. Ask the closing question as if it is inconceivable to you that the person could say anything but "Yes." Practice that approach. Practice the tone. Believe yourself, and so will others. Most of selling is not words; it is tone of voice and body language. Feel good, look good, act refined, and speak loudly. The person who speaks louder and clearer always dominates and wins. If you *want* to win, you will.

Attitude and attitude traits will determine success or failure in every business. If you incorporate these traits into your sales approach, the results are incredible. For example, you can break traits down into two areas: (1) supportive and positive traits and (2) reductive and negative traits. Supporting traits would be ambition, persuasiveness, initiative, self-direction ability, empathy, strong determination, key mental processes, versatility, tenacity, frankness, generosity, loyalty to yourself and your client, pride, self-confidence, self-control, self-reliance, sincerity, and humor. Negative traits would be deception, evasiveness, impulsiveness, weak-willed approach, argumentation, prejudice, lack of pride, lack of confidence, or, worst of all, fear of failure.

Joe Paterno, the famous college football coach, has said: "Success is a journey, and you must always do what you are afraid to do. To win, you must play as though you can't lose." All your closing techniques should be developed over time, through observation of others and experimentation. Keep in mind: "He only is exempt from failure who makes no effort." The difference between success and failure is a fine line. Success is filled with money, but failure stands alone. Remember, don't look back unless you want to go that way. Success is not the position you attain in life, but the obstacles you had to overcome to get there.

Break Through the Preoccupation Barrier

If people are wrestling with problems, they won't pay attention to you unless what you have to say is more important than their thoughts. One way to penetrate preoccupied minds is to help them solve their current problem. For example, you ask whether your prospect is planning a trip, and he or she describes a departure tomorrow to drive to a distant city. You can respond with your knowledge and suggestions for the fastest route. Your prospect's mind is then freer and more ready to turn attention to what you have to say. Had you jumped right into what you planned to say, his or her mind still would have been on the trip.

People do what they do because they feel comfortable acting that way. When someone's happy with the way things are, he or she has no reason to change. But if this same person becomes unhappy with circumstances, he or she will begin to feel uncomfortable. People don't like to feel uncomfortable; when they feel this way, they're open to suggestion. When they learn a new way to behave that removes the discomfort, they will gladly change their actions and be motivated to act in the new way.

The first step in sales is to make prospects feel uncomfortable about their *current* actions or circumstances. The second step is to show a new and better way to act that will remove their discomfort. Third, you need to stand aside and let them initiate change using their own free will. If you use these steps, you'll begin developing persuasive power that makes your calls pay off. At first, the process may seem a little involved, but as you follow the steps, they'll become more natural, and, before you know it, they'll become habit-forming.

Primitive peoples made fire without matches. First, they cut a pile of dry wood shavings. Then they struck two stones until they sparked and the shavings started to blaze. Getting through to other people is a similar process. First, you prepare a bed of attention. Then you strike a spark, and conversationally fan it until it creates a blaze of interest. To continue the comparison, a spark will burst into a fire faster when the wood shavings are dry and have not absorbed a lot of dampness. Similarly, a blaze of interest is created when the person's mind is "dry" and not absorbed with its own thoughts or emotions. Here are two ways for you to break down the most common mind absorbers that prevent you from getting the other person's attention.

Show Undivided Attention

Give the other person your undivided attention. Psychologists, psychiatrists, ministers, business managers, criminologists, and marriage counselors all have come to one simple conclusion about the art of dealing with people: If you really want to get results from an individual, you must master the art of giving that person your undivided attention.

It's the only way you can be sure of gaining power with people so you can get what *you* want, too.

Relieve Your Listener's Tensions

It is important to learn how to relieve your prospects' tensions. When prospects' nerves are tied in knots, their minds will be tied up, too. To get their full attention, you must first relieve their tensions.

One way to do this is to set an example by being relaxed yourself. Use a quiet, soft voice, slow and deliberate movements, and calm attentiveness toward prospects' personal needs and feelings. Actions like these create a relaxed atmosphere.

Keep the conversation safe. Don't discuss a topic that will aggravate or excite prospects. Talk about relaxing subjects, such as hobbies or plans for the coming weekend. There is one exception: If prospects are emotionally uptight about something in particular, it's often best to let them talk it out. When they have had a chance to vent their emotions, they will be more receptive to giving you complete attention.

Here's one narrative from an MDRT sales associate:

> I have to tell you about a million-dollar sale I opened and closed in 30 minutes using this technique. One day, a farmer client of mine walked into my office 30 minutes before lunchtime. Without an appointment, he sat down and, after the preliminaries, I asked him how I could help him. His response was that he wanted my advice whether to buy another farm for his son, who will be finishing school at the end of this year, or invest some money abroad because our country may be communist next year at this time! He was tensed up because he could lose everything he had built up during his lifetime. I asked questions and let him talk until his tension was down. Then I advised him to do both by buying the farm and investing money in a $1 million insurance policy. By doing so, I made him feel important.

The 80-15-5 Closing Rule

Have you ever found yourself trying desperately to convince a prospect to buy your products but eventually leaving without a sale? Your frustration level is extremely high, but so is that of the prospect. Too much time is spent talking about and teaching the effective techniques of closing a sale, when, in actual practice, the close of a sale should be the smallest portion of the time that you spend with the prospect.

Learn to use the 80-15-5 rule:

✓ 80 percent of the time is spent on fact finding—uncovering, exploring, and developing problems the prospect has.

✓ 15 percent is spent on developing possible solutions.

✓ 5 percent is spent on the close.

High-pressure sales professionals, unfortunately, turn this formula around. They spend 15 percent of the sales presentation uncovering and developing the problems, 5 percent in solutions, and 80 percent in closing. Certain selling processes represent the clearest examples of this reversed formula. These processes provide minimum solutions to closing sales, negate sizable commission opportunities, and create a barrier between prospects and sales professionals.

Selling is educating. Most MDRT sales professionals strongly believe that closing a sale is done by properly educating their clients. They ask: What are the clients' needs? What are the possible solutions to these needs? Which solution is the best? When the 80–15–5 rule is followed, you carefully spend your time defining problems and developing possible solutions—and the best solution becomes obvious. Thus, the close simply says: "If the goals and needs are accurate and if you agree that this solution is the best, then let's get the product in your possession." The sale is completed early in the counseling process; getting payment for your products or services is then merely a formality. By the time you get to the decision area and an action-checklist page, your prospects will know what needs to be done to solve their problems.

When customers are being billed for your services, they pay very close attention and they do what you recommend. But you must be patient and resist the temptation to close too early. You cannot take shortcuts and close before your prospects' problems are clearly identified and the suggested solutions are carefully analyzed. In some cases, the closing process can take four to six weeks, but the results are well worth it!

Be patient: The sales process is mostly an educational process. If you follow the 80–15–5 Rule, you will not experience the widespread frustration of being unable to close a sale. In a counselor role, you will have the trust of your prospects. They will listen carefully, do what you feel is best, and follow your recommendations. The compensation to you can be significant. Not only will you be paid for your services, but you will solidify your role as a caring sales professional. You will then be on the receiving end of countless referrals and return-customer business.

Motivation in the Close

"No, I'm sorry, but it's just not possible tonight—we can't go out. I have too much work to do at home," a husband told his wife, who wanted to see a much-talked-about movie—but, through her persistence, they went anyway!

"Buying new office computers is out of the question this year," the manager told his support staff—but, again, through persistence, they changed his thinking and the office soon had new computers!

"Fat chance it can be done," the coach of the last-place team said hopelessly, when he reviewed his chances of beating the undefeated, powerhouse team—but his team pulled an upset and won!

Impossible things are being accomplished every day, but only by people who want to win—and only when their motivation is strong enough to smash through any obstacles that stand in their way.

The purchase of the products and services you are selling frequently looks impossible to prospects who look at their budgets, and at the cost of living, and say, "It's just out of the question." At this point, many fine sales presentations collapse. Sales professionals become oversympathetic and accept their prospects' statements. This is the "D" day, the "H" hour, the crisis point in the sale. Facts, figures, illustrations, and analysis of needs are all essentials in laying the foundation for action, but the interview with any prospect is going to be just so much conversation unless the sales professional can motivate action—immediately.

Halting the Pendulum

As prospects waver between decision and indecision, it is as if a pendulum were swinging back and forth in their minds. "Yes, it's an excellent product or service you are selling," the prospect says, and the pendulum swings toward decision to act, "but I just don't see how I can . . ." and the pendulum swings back to indecision.

"Yes, the product would meet my needs . . . but there are so many others to choose from . . . ," and the pendulum goes through another cycle. Those are agonizing pauses for the salesperson. What is needed is a way to stop the pendulum at the point where prospects recognize the benefits, and before the thousands of reasons for not buying your products or services flood back into their minds. Let's consider some ways to stop the pendulum.

Some sales professionals seek to stop the pendulum by applying pressure. Much has been said about pressure selling, and there are so many misconceptions about pressure and prospects' reactions to it that we need to explore this subject a bit further.

A sales professional can't force any prospect to buy. Most people to whom the sales professional sells are sensitive and respectable, and any attempt to force them to buy will surely create resistance and hostility. But the pendulum has to be stopped. One way to do this is to get the prospect rather than the sales professional to initiate the pressure. This is the purpose of motivation and delivering motivating stories.

People buy what they want from people whom they like. It is up to the sales professional to make suggestions so logical and so appealing that the prospect will want to buy. The prospect must be emotionally concerned. Logic tells the prospect that your products or services are necessary. Emotions tell the prospect that they are necessary right now.

Do you have the right to motivate?

Strong closers are people of conviction. They believe implicitly in their product or service, and, through their enthusiasm, they convert others. The reason some salespeople have found it difficult to use motivation in their sales efforts is: They themselves lack any deep-seated belief in the value of the products or services that they are offering.

Sales professionals should look first at their own convictions. Do they honestly believe what they preach? "I am not my brother's keeper, but I can show this person what this product or service has done for others." The motivating story, like every other type of close, has its roots in the interview. The sales professional's story is wasted—or actually harmful—if not told in the proper place.

True motivation is not a last-minute appendix tacked on to the conclusion of a sales presentation. True motivation is built into the entire sales procedure by the sales professional's own convictions as much as by what is said. The motivation of conviction creates both momentum and a mood, and they make the actual motivating story a natural climax to all that has gone before.

Here's a true story: A sales professional was once called into his company's headquarters for temporary duty on the staff that trains new sales associates. The school session lasted for two weeks. Most of the instructor's time was spent with a small number of students. In the classroom, they were grouped together around a large table. Day after day, the salesperson/instructor unfolded the story of how to use his company's products and their functions to the interested audience. It was an intimate, informal, friendly session.

While working with class after class of new sales associates, the instructor noticed an interesting phenomenon. Although no attempt was made during the two weeks to sell the students the company's products, they almost invariably ended the two-week session by voluntarily making a purchase. What was the reason? Three months' minimum field experience was required to qualify for the school. So all of the students had been exposed to the needs for the company's products. These new sales associates bought because:

✓ They accepted the instructor who was known and respected by them.

✓ They accepted what was said because they knew that the instructor's single objective was to help them.

✓ Through sincerity and enthusiasm, the instructor's convictions about the company's products were transmitted to them.

✓ Through the experience of the instructor, the students were able to relate the products to their own personal needs and were motivated to the extent that they wanted these products enough to buy them voluntarily.

Did the sales professional's convictions and enthusiasm throughout the entire two-week class recreate, to some degree, a classroom atmosphere in which the students couldn't help but buy? The answer is unequivocally "Yes"!

What Stories Can You Tell?

The object of motivation is to secure action—buying action—and to secure it now. Motivation does not imply that the prospect

must get sentimental about the products or services you are selling; rather, he or she gets sensible about them. This is in harmony
with the overall purpose of making it easy for the prospect to
buy. As the prospect sees your products or services in their
proper perspective and realizes that they offer the best way to
meet immediate needs, reaching a decision becomes easier. The
salesperson gets the prospect thinking about doing what they
both know is best.

There are several sources of good motivating stories; the
most important sources are your own experiences. You should
never hesitate to tell your own stories—whatever they may be.
The stories that come from your own experience are easiest to
tell and sound most natural. If you don't have a positive firsthand
story about how a client used your products or services, perhaps
an associate can share with you some direct benefits he or she
has experienced. Nothing that a sales professional reads in a
book can take the place of actually watching your products and
services at work.

The story need not be highly dramatic. A simple narrative is
often most effective. You can look back on your own career.
There may have been a number of instances when your products
or services came to the rescue of an individual or company when
they needed them the most. One of those instances may be the
very reason that you're still in the business today.

Even when the story is a personal one, it should be written
out and carefully rehearsed, again and again, until you can tell
it easily and naturally. This will help to overcome any doubt
that you may have about your ability to tell a motivating story
well. Preparation and rehearsal have another advantage. They
reduce the hazard that you will get so carried away in telling
your story that you'll add detail after detail until the point of
the story is lost.

In addition to reviewing your own experiences, you should talk to other people who have felt the influence of your products and services. Why do your customers own your products and recommend them to their friends and associates? These are stories in themselves.

Chapter 4

Anticipating and Handling Objections

Fear of objections has ruined many sales careers, yet the best salespeople know that objections are a normal part of the sales process. If they are prepared for, objections can actually work in the salesperson's favor by serving as closing clues. MDRT sales professionals close with confidence, as this chapter illustrates.

Handling Objections

Beware of prospects or customers who fail to ask questions or to raise objections to your sales proposition. Such individuals are usually the hardest prospects to sell. Why? Because it is the most natural thing in the world for prospects to question and object. Skilled sales professionals welcome both responses as evidence of genuine interest—when they are sincerely expressed. Whatever the product or service, whoever the buyer or prospect, welcome any objections and questions. They are a prospect's way of saying, "Yes, I'm interested in what you have to say, but I have some mental reservations that are blocking my acceptance of your proposition. Remove them and you can close your sale." Always maintain a positive attitude toward this evidence of sales resistance.

What can a sales professional do, in addition to maintaining a positive attitude, to overcome objections? To answer this question, we will discuss, in sequence, the most favorable time to answer objections, the techniques you can employ, and the ways you can answer specific objections. We will assume in our discussion that your prospect has both a use for your product or service and the means to pay.

The Right Time to Answer

Most sales professionals, when asked to pick the best time to answer objections, will respond rather quickly, "Immediately." This is often the case, but there are other, more suitable, times to help customers hurdle the obstacles. Four different approaches are described here. Choose the one that is appropriate for the facts in a particular situation.

1. Anticipate the objection.

The best time to answer objections—with one notable exception—is before they are raised. This can readily be done with common objections that you know—from your own or your company's experience—will frequently reappear. The principal exception to this rule is a situation in which sales professionals have an answer so powerful that they purposely wait for the prospect to raise the objection instead of answering it in advance. In such a situation, you may be well rewarded for your skillful timing. The answer you give may move the presentation to a point where the close itself may be at hand.

For example, a sales professional has carefully driven a prospect around a new housing development and has walked the prospect through a house that the prospect especially likes. The sales professional has secured the prospect's approval on all the items of major importance. The sales professional knows from experience, however, that the prospect will raise an objection about the lack of shopping facilities. Rather than anticipate the objection, the sales professional waits for the prospect to bring it up. When the prospect says, "Well, I like the house and the location, but there is nowhere to shop in the immediate or surrounding area," the sales professional answers, "I can understand your saying that. I would feel the same. You'll be glad to know that a contract has already been signed for the building of a modern shopping center close by."

Alert sales professionals always compile a list of the troublesome objections they meet most frequently. Then they prepare the most effective answers that they can truthfully give, and they weave them into their sales presentation. This minimizes the number of objections that prospects can raise. The prospects are denied the chance to put the sales professional on the defensive by raising objections, for they will have been answered already.

2. Answer the objection immediately.

The answers to some objections will not have been anticipated in your presentation. *Whenever sincere objections are raised by prospects, an immediate answer should be given.* Not to do so, except in the situations to be discussed below, is to risk prospects' questioning your ability to respond. There is another good reason for answering a sincere objection immediately: When sales professionals hold off the answer to an honest objection, prospects often focus their minds on this particular problem, to the exclusion of anything else that is brought up. If such a mental fixation occurs, sales professionals have compromised and weakened the entire sales presentation; they may well have lost the confidence and faith of the prospect.

The following example illustrates the lesson. A customer was looking carefully at an expensive, advanced-model 35mm camera. He was heard to say, in an earnest, questioning way, "[Sales

Professional's Name], that new shutter, is it . . . ?" The sales professional, obviously interested in only his own story, replied with the briefest "It's great," and continued with a monologue about the camera. Again the customer tried to get in a word about the shutter. Totally ignored, he focused his eyes on the shutter and stood still as the sales professional prattled on with the camera story. But something must have finally penetrated the sales professional's brain, and he launched a trial balloon: "Did you want to use our regular time payment plan or . . . ?" It was, finally, the customer's turn. "[Sales Professional's Name], I didn't hear a word you said. All I wanted to know was about that shutter!" And with that, he hastened away.

3. *Delay your answer.*

There are two situations in which it is important to delay your answer to the objection: (1) when the objection is not related to the point under consideration, and (2) when price is queried before your value story has been developed. Here's what to say in the first situation: "[Prospect's Name], the question you ask is a sensible one. In fact, I plan to discuss it carefully, in connection with another feature, in just a moment. At this point, I want to be certain you are familiar with the design features we have just discussed." (Don't pause—get right back into the sales presentation.)

In the second situation—the early price question—experienced sales professionals hold off until the value story is built. Here's how:

SALES PROFESSIONAL (selling office equipment to Prospect): "No question, [Prospect's Name], price is always important. You will agree, however, that unless this machine can provide the savings in time and the economy of operation that you want—well, you wouldn't be interested at *any* price. Before we think about price, let's see what this machine can do for you." (Proceed immediately into the sales presentation; don't pause.)

Sales professionals may occasionally quote prices early in the sale, after attention and interest have been secured, and when they know that the price of their product or service is considerably higher than the prospect has targeted for this purchase. This is what to say:

SALES PROFESSIONAL: "Yes, [Prospect's Name], the price is quite high. It may seem substantial, but I can and will conclusively show you that it is worth that and more." (Go right into the sales presentation again, without any pause. Just brush it off.)

4. Ignore the objection.

If possible, ignore the objection when it is of little worth or significance. If it is brought up a second time, you have to answer it. Again, don't be like the camera sales professional! The technique of ignoring objections should be used sparingly, and only in instances where the flimsiest type of excuse is being offered by the prospect.

Techniques for Answering Objections

Certain tested techniques are of inestimable value and can be used in answering objections and questions. Practice these until you are completely familiar with them and can use them easily and perfectly. The discussion and dialogues below are premised on two conditions: (1) the prospects have funds available, and (2) they have a genuine need for your product or service.

The following techniques will be explained and illustrated:

✓ Indirect or "Yes-But."

✓ Boomerang.

✓ Offset.

✓ Question.

✓ Direct denial.

In a specific sales situation, one of these techniques will be more effective than the others. Whatever your method of answering, be certain that you have listened carefully and courteously to what the prospect has said. Although you may have heard the same objection from others, make the prospect feel, through your actions and your answer, that it is being thoughtfully considered and that you respect his or her opinion. Above all, after you have answered the objection, leave it and move on to the next point in your presentation. Don't complicate your presentation by magnifying a molehill of an objection into a mountainous obstacle. Never make your prospect feel foolish by maintaining an air that is haughty, arrogant, or contemptuous. That is the surest way to cut off the prospect's flow of questions, which are your guideposts to progress.

Indirect or "Yes-But" Technique

It is said that a soft answer turns away wrath. This is probably the reason you will find yourself using this technique more than any other. It is the finest method for dulling the sharpness of an objection or for postponing or flanking it. The indirect method is most frequently used in combination with one of the other recommended techniques. It is a way to avoid flatly contradicting the prospect.

SALES PROFESSIONAL: "I can understand your feeling this way; others whom I have visited have felt the same. The last six years, however, have proved that the new plastic will withstand as much heat, or even more heat, as any type of glass presently manufactured."

Boomerang Technique

This is sometimes called the "turnabout-response" or "reverse-English" method. The sales professional who uses this method throws the prospects' objections back at them as the very reason for buying. The sales professional in effect says to the prospect, "That's the most powerful reason for you to choose this product!" Whenever you are presented with an opportunity to apply this technique, you will find it effective.

PROSPECT (to sales professional who has called to explain the home painting service plan of his company): ". . . but I can't afford to paint this house."

SALES PROFESSIONAL: "I'm more pleased to have you say that than any other remark you could make. That is because I know that if you couldn't afford to invest so nominal a sum in a house painting job, you could hardly afford to pay for a repair bill that would be many times that sum after another hard winter without it."

Alternately:

PROSPECT: "I'm too busy to see you."

SALES PROFESSIONAL: "I've come to see you because you *are* busy. If you weren't, our service wouldn't interest you."

Offset Technique

The offset or superior point/fact technique admits the validity of the prospect's objection and then stresses a superior point that more than compensates for it. The sales professional capitalizes on the fact that no single product can be all things to all people. If the sales professional is selling a car with an automatic shift to a customer who objects that it is not economical, the sales professional might say, "It does get a little less mileage to the gallon. But that expense will be more than made up by the extra trade-in allowance you will get on your next car." If the gold mountings being shown to a retail jeweler are lighter than others, the sales professional stresses the lower price per mounting and what this can mean to sales. If the customer objects to a higher price, the sales professional points out the features and services that justify it. This technique does not remove the objection; rather, it directs the prospect's attention to an offsetting advantage. Although it is not used as much as the other techniques, there are situations in which it can be used to great advantage.

Question Technique

With this method, the sales professional asks the question—a reversal of the usual prospect–sales professional relationship. Used in a sincere manner to encourage prospects to talk, it is a technique that can prove most valuable. Not only does it stimulate prospects to respond by asking them a question—even one that consists of the single word "Why?"—but it also helps to clarify prospects' thinking and affords the sales professional time for deciding on an effective answer. The use of a question to answer an objection sometimes helps prospects answer their own objection, because the prospects are required to defend and justify their own position. Here is an example:

PROSPECT: "I like the item you have, but I don't want anything to do with the company you represent."

SALES PROFESSIONAL: "Certainly I appreciate your frankness, but I would be grateful if you helped me. What has occurred in the past that makes you feel this way toward the company?" (The prospect then goes on to explain what has been annoying him; the sales professional listens, and prepares an effective answer to the objection.)

PROSPECT: "I know that I can get other business services for less."

SALES PROFESSIONAL: "Well, tell me, [Prospect's Name], what is it that you want in a business service—are you really interested only in the cost?"

PROSPECT: "No one is. I'm interested in how it can help to improve my plant operation." (Here, the sales professional has used his own questioning technique to lead the prospect to answer the objection.)

Direct Denial Technique

This method flatly contradicts prospects' objections. It directly tells the customers that they are wrong. There are times when its use is justified, but it can be used only by those with wide experience. When the prospect offers an absolutely incorrect objection about your product or service, or attacks you or your company with a severely derogatory observation, the direct denial may well prove the only satisfactory means to meet the situation adequately. Employ caution in using it, however, to avoid seriously offending the prospect or customer; otherwise, the prospect's antagonism is aroused and the chances for further arguments are enhanced. Most of the time, you are probably better off using some variation of the "Yes-But" technique.

PROSPECT: "Your cleaner has only a ⅛-horsepower motor."

SALES PROFESSIONAL: "Actually, it has a ¼-horsepower motor. My company has never made one with less because no vacuum with a smaller motor could do the job required of it."

Alternatively:

PROSPECT: "The company you represent certainly has never kept its word. Any service guarantees it offers are hardly worth the paper they are printed on."

SALES PROFESSIONAL: "Actually, [Prospect's Name], the facts that I will present to you are evidence that this just isn't true. For over 40 years, our company has built a reputation for service—service that has provided satisfaction for our customers. We will write a service guarantee, specifically tailored to your needs, into your contract."

Answering Objections Raised by Prospects

The key to the successful handling of objections lies in the sales professional's ability to distinguish between two types of objections: (1) excuse or "stall" objections, which aim to help prospects avoid either hearing the sales professional's propositions or making a purchasing decision; and (2) sincere objections that are an evidence of real interest in sales propositions. The distinction between these two main groups of objections is obvious when outlined here, but, on many actual sales occasions, a distinction cannot be quickly and positively drawn. The very same statement, "I'm too busy now," may be made by two different prospects. For Prospect A, it will represent an excuse to avoid hearing your proposition; for Prospect B, the statement will be an honest objection. Prospect B may actually have other obligations that prevent a meeting with you. Your own judgment, developed through experience, is the only reliable basis for distinguishing between the two. This discussion can only show you these two levels of prospects' behavior and provide identifying characteristics.

Thus, for the purpose of analysis, objections are treated as belonging to two main groups: excuses and stalls, and genuine objections.

Excuses and Stalls

The seven excuses and stalls most frequently presented by prospects are offered here. Remember that any objection, under certain conditions, can be genuine. Therefore, the discussion of each one will consider both types of situations and will show the techniques to be employed when the objection is actually an excuse and when it is a bona fide objection.

1. "I would like to think this over."

This statement is sometimes expressed in different ways: "I want to look around," or "I can't decide now." Each answer, if stated as an excuse objection, is an effort by prospects to avoid a situation that would lead to a decision. Many prospects will go to extremes of evasion. When prospects deliver some version of this statement, a question such as "Is there any other reason for waiting?" or "Is that your only reason?" can be most helpful. If a prospect replies in the negative, the sales professional proceeds to show, by use of an actual case history or anecdote, that delay can only mean postponement of the savings, profit, and other benefits that can be reaped right now. If the prospect claims to have still other reasons, probe further, unearth the real reason for the hesitation, and make an effort to remove it. Alternatively, this excuse objection can be simply ignored as you continue to describe positive factors to gain the prospect's conviction.

There will be some prospects who honestly must have time to think your proposition over. Others may feel that they must look around or be shown comparable items that are available. On that assumption, and only then, you can say, "I thoroughly understand how important this purchase is to you. That is why I strongly suggest that in thinking over your decision (or looking at any other similar product), you look carefully at the advantages to be found in this product." The sales professional then creates a blueprint in detail, by comparisons or summary, and presents the main facts in the proposition that would make it the prospect's wisest choice. The sales professional must always arrange a return appointment, because it is thereby assumed by both parties that the prospect will not come to a final decision until after their next meeting. This gives the sales professional an opportunity to reinforce the prospect's conviction regarding the proposition.

2. *"I would prefer to discuss this with. . . ."*

You will frequently receive this reply when there are two or more owners in the business. This excuse is most convenient for prospects to use early in a meeting, to indicate that it is a waste of time to discuss any proposition, since no decision could possibly be made without the partner's consent. In industrial selling, the design person may have to be present. For our purposes, let us suppose that the prospect has indicated a need to talk with a partner. The sales professional answers, "Yes, I know you want to talk this over with your partner; but your partner will want your opinion as well. This is why I would first like your opinion so that, since you are more familiar with this phase of the operation, you can judge the merits of my product. Then I will explain the proposition to your partner. If there are any questions, you can fill your partner in on the details."

If the need for discussion with the other party is real, the objection is no longer treated as an excuse, and efforts are made to arrange an appointment at which both partners can be present. In such circumstances, make certain that you quickly discover which individual is the dominant personality. Then speak to both partners, but direct your strongest appeals to the dominant one.

3. *"I am too busy now."*

This can be a real objection—and not an unusual one. When it is genuine, simply make arrangements for another time that will be mutually more convenient. However, many postponements can be avoided by the prior arrangement of an appointment.

If this is an excuse objection, the sales professional can say, "That's the very reason I called to see you, [Prospect's Name]. It is because you are so busy that my proposition will be of genuine interest to you." Another answer that is often given to this type of excuse objection is, "I'm sure that you will agree you are never too busy to look at a product that will give you [specifies dollars and cents] in profits—*extra* profits, each week of the year." Once this excuse objection has been handled, the sales professional is ready to begin the sales presentation and persuade the prospect that everything claimed can come true.

One other situation should be mentioned here. When prospects are busy at their desks, you can say, "[Prospect's Name], because you are busy—as am I—I will not take more than 10 minutes of your time. If, at the end of that period, you are not honestly interested, I will leave. And I mean just that." Without further delay, you begin the sales presentation.

4. *"I cannot afford to buy now."*

The excuse objection that a sales professional will hear most often is: "I can't afford it." In response, the sales professional can most effectively use the boomerang method, making the objection the very reason for the purchase. If the prospect, for instance, levels the can't-afford-it objection at your proposition, you have only to answer, "That is the very reason you can't afford to be without the product [or service] I am selling."

Naturally, some prospects and customers honestly cannot afford to purchase your product or service. These individuals should not be persuaded to buy. Under no conditions should you ever overload prospects or customers beyond what you honestly believe they can afford, either in dollars or in inventory.

5. "I am simply not interested."

Whenever you hear this objection—whether it's an excuse or the truth—take stock of yourself as a sales professional; you have probably failed to secure the attention of your prospect by proper use of the techniques suggested earlier. Make a note to re-analyze the interest-getter you have been using. Meanwhile, there are ways of meeting this objection. If it is an excuse objection, the "Yes-But" technique can sometimes be used to good advantage, but soft-pedal the "Yes" element: "[Prospect's Name], I know you will be interested in the case history of a plant whose owner you know well and whose situation was quite similar to yours." You then proceed to relate the anecdote and to prove the merits of the proposition rapidly. The aim, of course, is to show the prospect that his or her situation is not unique, and that a solution others have used may well be appropriate.

There will be people who simply are not interested, and no action on the part of the sales professional can or will change their minds.

6. "I am satisfied with my present source."

The sales professional can frequently answer this, with positive results, if it is an excuse objection. The sales professional says, "Yes, I can well understand that your present connections are excellent. However, I'm sure that you would not want to overlook the chance to add a line [or an additional source of material] that can add an extra [dollar amount] profit each month [or, in the case of a raw material, ensure an uninterrupted supply]." The sales professional emphasizes to prospects that they are not expected to cease relations with their present sources. It is merely being suggested that the prospects share some of this business for their own best interests.

Where this is a real objection and the addition of your product would be duplication, there is a real problem. The best solution that can be recommended, if it is justified, is to show the prospect (usually a retailer or distributor) that both lines can be stocked side-by-side. The records would then indicate which is doing the better job. Or, you might prove that different customer preferences justify carrying both. If you are selling industrial supplies, you can show what was suggested earlier: Two sources are better than one.

7. *"I have a friend or relative in the business."*

This is, in most cases, an excuse by prospects either to discourage you from calling on them or, if you are already face-to-face, to close off your interview. Prospects may have a friend or relative in the business, but this excuse objection is not going to result in any purchase; they actually have no intention of buying at all if they can avoid it. The "Yes-But" approach is best here: "You are certainly to be admired for your loyalty, [Prospect's Name]. I wish more people placed a real value on their friendships. However, sometimes I wonder, and perhaps you have too, if we can expect as much from our friends as we can from those who approach us as genuinely interested strangers with a completely objective viewpoint. At one time or another, you may not have wanted others, especially those whom you know intimately, to be familiar with matters that are particularly personal to you."

The sales professional can then show how, because of an honest and eager desire to help, the proposed product can better serve the prospect. "If my product and the service I can offer to back it up don't stand up well in comparison, then I don't deserve to have your business."

There are, of course, special situations where sales cannot be made because this relationship is genuine and the objection cannot be removed.

Genuine Objections

Real objections—whether directed at your product or service, your company, or yourself—require that you provide the prospect with a positive and satisfying answer. The seven genuine objections described below are related directly to your proposition, so you must strive to get the prospect's agreement. These objections must be answered if the decision to purchase is not to be postponed.

1. The price level.

"What is a cynic? A man who knows the price of everything and the value of nothing." But the average prospect is not a cynic, and Oscar Wilde's shrewd observation in *Lady Windermere's Fan* should be transmuted, in your sales professional's lexicon, into something like, "Good prospects are people who want to know the price of everything in relation to its value to them." People are far more concerned with attributes such as style, quality, and durability. Such values often come first.

Show them these values—as we have demonstrated time and again—and they will buy your product or service. No one would question that price, at some time and in some manner, is a part of every business transaction, but remember that it is rarely *all there is* to selling.

You should have the same constructive attitude toward price that you have toward your product. Be convinced in your own mind that the price is right, and convey your conviction to the prospect with a tone of assurance. Only then can you expect that your prospect's attitude will also be positive. Some methods of approach to the price objection can be most helpful. These include suggestions on when to quote price; what to do if the buyer says, "The price is too high"; dealing with a "cut-your-price" buyer; meeting the comparison-price problem; and arranging a trade-in. Never sell price; sell value. Never overcome price; enhance value.

The most advantageous time to quote price is after you have had a full opportunity to build up the value story for your product or service. By the time you have secured the prospects' interest, stimulated their desire, and secured their confidence, your demonstration will have made value outweigh price. There is one situation that may make it advantageous to quote your price early in the sale—right after attention and interest have been secured: when you know the price of your product or service is considerably higher than the amount the prospect had in mind for such a product or service. In such a case, you can say, "Yes, [Prospect's Name], the price of this item is [dollar amount]. It may seem a substantial sum to pay, but I can show you conclusively that it is worth what is asked—and more." Without any hesitation, you then develop the presentation. Freed from worrying about the prospect's fear of the price, you build a value story that makes cost recede and accents the desire for the product. In most cases, as we have pointed out, the best procedure is to build the value story first and then quote the price.

If the buyer says, "The price is too high," you must revert to specific means. Many sales professionals, particularly those who are new to the selling field, hold that their prices *are* too high, and their negative attitude is often conveyed to prospects. Small wonder that the prospects balk! In most cases, the fault lies with the sales presentation, not with the price. If prospects have been given a sound value story in terms of their own best interest, such situations would never arise. Today, we have a quality market and, if you always make it a point to demonstrate the fine features of the product or service that you are selling, this difficulty will often be overcome.

To prospects who say, "Your price is too high," demonstrate the many benefits and features of your product in a positive manner. Show them why your product is so good that customers are willing to pay more. Emphasize to the customers that you get what you pay for, and that in the long run they will receive far more value for their money in buying the higher-priced item. As often as it has been repeated, John Ruskin's famous advice is still sound: "There is hardly anything in the world that some men cannot make a little worse and sell a little cheaper, and the people who consider price only are this man's lawful prey."

Another method is helpful when this objection is offered: Break the price down into small units. To tell prospects simply that the cost of painting their home is X dollars is to make price the primary consideration. But when you say to prospects, "This quality paint job means you will not have to paint for at least five years. At a yearly cost of [dollar amount], less than [dollar amount] per week, you will preserve a home that cost many thousands of dollars, a home you plan to live in with your family for years to come. That's not much to spend to protect so important an investment, is it?"

Whenever buyers say, "The price is too high," ask yourself whether you built a sound, value-packed sales story that forced them to minimize the importance of the price. Make certain that you have shown the profit in dollars, or the satisfaction that will be theirs, when they own your product or use your service.

Every sales professional will, at one time or another, face prospects who haggle over a quoted price in an effort to get a lower quotation. Here again, if you have quoted your price with confidence based on a value story and have not indicated any possibility of a lower one, much of the force of their attempt to bargain has been removed. An appeal to their sense of fair play can also have an effect. Tell them: "[Prospect's Name], our company has always prided itself on one thing: We have one price on this item for every one of our customers. I'm certain that you would not want to feel when I left here that someone else could get a better price than you. You will never have any occasion to think this." And then reiterate the features of the product being offered. This objection can also be minimized by never quoting a price and leaving it suspended in the air without support. When you quote your price, always do it this way: "Yes, the price for this is [dollar amount], and this includes the labor and the service. It is a quality product with features that no one else can offer." This method emphasizes what prospects receive and directs their attention away from the price.

Some prospects may object: "Your competitor sells the same product for less." Suppose the prospects' statement is not true, although they may honestly believe it is. In this case, your task is to find out the facts that are responsible for this attitude. By skillful questioning, direct the prospect's attention to your product, and make the comparison. "Did you see the same number of bearings in the other machine? Was it mounted on five points to eliminate any vibration, as this machine is? Frequently, two machines may look the same, but their performances will be quite different." This is the recommended procedure; it is preferable to issuing a direct denial that can only antagonize the buyer. If the statement is true, you can also point out certain additional advantages, such as terms, service, delivery, or reputation, that justify the decision to buy from you. Emphasize that these factors should far outweigh any slight price differences that may exist.

2. The trade-in allowance.

Many products—such as appliances, industrial machinery and equipment, and office equipment—require sales professionals to sell prospects on the trade-in allowance that can be offered for an older model, as well as on the desirability of the new model. Coping with the trade-in problem requires that the sales professional have an ability to evaluate, and tact in stating the allowance that can be made. If the sales professional makes too liberal a trade-in, the profit in selling the new item is compromised, or in some cases, eliminated entirely. If the evaluation is too low, customers will shop around and will naturally buy from a competing firm that offers more. There is a middle ground: The trade-in should be handled honestly, and a fair price should be offered to prospects. All too frequently, the sales professionals who have difficulty in reaching agreements on trade-in allowances have created their own problem. When the need arises to evaluate, they take a cursory look at the item—often make some harsh remark in an effort to deprecate the prospect's trade-in—and then wonder why the prospect is offended and not receptive to the recommendation. Here are some suggestions that should be of real assistance to you in dealing with this problem.

When you have a trade-in to consider as a part of your sale, always present the value story on the new product before a valuation is placed on the old. Most sales professionals will not have a liberal trade-in policy (at least the prospect will rarely feel it is liberal enough), so the point becomes even more important. Under these conditions, experienced sales professionals maximize their efforts to present their product in such a manner that the prospect's desire for the new is heightened to a point of eager want. Only then do they place a value on the used article. Never begin by selling the allowance; first sell your product. You might say to the customer who immediately asks about the trade-in allowance, "[Prospect's Name], of course we're going to give you the benefit of a good allowance on your used machine. However, I'm certain that you will first want to look at the new equipment to see all of the features that it has to meet your job demands." You then immediately launch into a demonstration of the new machine.

There is one more point that sales professionals often neglect in a trade-in situation: The value of the trade-in must be proven as conclusively as the merits of the new product. This can be done by using a very simple procedure. Instead of making the evaluation after a cursory look at the used item, try to get an idea of what the prospects expect on the old model. The prospects' idea of what they should get will usually be higher than what can or should be allowed, and your problem then is to convince them that you are offering everything possible. This is where you can use an appraisal sheet (which may be supplied by the company or may be of your own invention) to good advantage. An appraisal sheet is a list of items needed to recondition old machines. You then write down the things that will have to be done in order to make the trade-in item salable. In your portfolio, carry a list of current book prices in the trade for the various pieces of equipment. Tactfully, even before stating your price, show the prospects what has to be done, reminding them that they too would expect these things in a piece of used equipment. What have you accomplished? For one thing, you have proven to them that your evaluation was not haphazard, and you have instilled some confidence in your judgment. You have also postponed committing yourself on an allowance figure until you have prepared them for a realistic amount. When this figure has been balanced against quoted market figures for a piece of equipment in condition similar to that of the one they own, you have proved your story.

If the prospects insist that they can get a better trade-in on a competitive piece of equipment, you can show them that some manufacturers are prepared to give larger trade-in allowances than a situation justifies, because they have to. Point out that the amount they seem to have gained, and more, will probably be lost on their next trade. Or you can, in many cases, prove that the additional quality and service that your company offers more than justify the difference. Above all, remember that you are selling two things whenever there is a trade-in: a new unit and an allowance on the old. Always sell the new before you value the old. Naturally, when possible, it is best for the sales professional to have the appraisal made by a third person.

3. Adequate stock.

This is an objection voiced most frequently by retailers, and occasionally by industrial consumers. The sales professional is advised by prospects or customers that they have sufficient stock on hand for the present and they can't hope to handle any more. Sometimes, this is used as an excuse or stall; at other times, it is a very real objection. In the case of retailers, every sales professional knows that they have a primary interest: larger profits. And where do they get their profits? From the relationship of two factors: cost of goods sold divided by average inventory at cost—in a word, turnover. The fact that all items do not have the same rate of turnover is the key to answering this objection. Your task is to show prospects, with supporting facts and figures, that, if they stock your line, they will have products that provide substantial turnover and the profits that go with it. In a tactful manner, demonstrate that the prospects are overstocked with items that are not moving. Remind them that no merchant can ever overstock by taking in a line that moves off the shelf and into the hands of customers. Industrial overstocking, where supplies are managed by professional buyers and executives, is usually due to conditions beyond the control of either the prospect or the sales professional. You might search for reliable information on some impending event that would make further stocking-up advisable, but under no circumstances should this means be used either to answer an objection or as a closing technique if it is not your well-informed opinion that the suggested interference with supply or the rise in price will take place.

4. Product quality.

The most effective way to avoid price competition is to sell quality. Always think of quality as represented by the sum total of the characteristics that make your product or service a value. Even if your product is priced lower, you must show that the quality is right in terms of the price paid: "Yes, [Prospect's Name], there is no single product that can be all things to all people, but this one with its low price offers more value benefits than any other on the market. Let me show you. . . ." On the other hand, if the product or service is priced higher, demonstrate the superior quality that more than compensates for the extra dollars spent in both the short and the long run: "[Prospect's Name], there is a very old saying, 'You get what you pay for,' and I'm sure you know it to be true from your own personal experience. Over the long term, and even in the short run, you're getting much more, dollar for dollar, by selecting this better quality. It's a superior value!"

Again, remember that increased income levels, coupled with an appreciation for better things, provide you, the sales professional, with a splendid opportunity to sell better merchandise by emphasizing increased value and better performance. You will find this especially easy to do if you follow what was said early in this text: Pick a product or service to sell because you firmly believe in its superior qualities. Then, even the products in your lower-priced lines will provide buyer satisfaction.

5. Dissatisfaction with your service.

These objections will include criticisms of credit policy, shipments, adjustments, maintenance and repair service, advertising, and any other service rendered by the company you represent.

Some of these objections will be volunteered by prospects; others will require skillful questioning to give you a clear picture of what is disturbing them. If the prospects claim that your credit terms are not long enough, prove to them, by the experiences of others, that your goods will sell so readily that long-term credit is not needed. If shipments are slow, show them that they are arriving as fast as possible under prevailing conditions.

Adjustment problems are best handled directly through your office whenever possible. If you are faced with this difficulty, extreme tact is needed. The best approach is to let the customers unburden themselves; then strive to settle the matter for your company and your customer in an equitable manner.

Objections to maintenance and repair service should be answered by carefully pointing out that your company is most concerned with this element of customer satisfaction. Explain the amount and kinds of service your company makes available; detail any time limits and changes essential to the service. Handle this type of objection most carefully—it may determine the final closing of the sale. Always remember that competition and standardization have sometimes tended to minimize differences between products. Better service may swing the sale.

If customers object because you do not have an advertising program, try to sell them on the merits of your product and suggest means that will better merchandise the various items. Personally assisting in interior and exterior display activities, and even selling on the floor, may help to prove how well your product will sell without advertising in the various media. Do not deceive prospects with advertising plans that you know will never be available.

6. Prejudices toward your company.

Prejudices may include reservations about a company's financial stability, background, policies, and personnel. If you are a sales professional for a smaller concern that does comparatively little advertising, you may meet this type of objection often. Experienced sales professionals are not disturbed by these objections, for they have already anticipated them. They carry portfolio material that offers proof of their company's financial stability. To prospects who have never heard of their company or its background, they will explain: "[Prospect's Name], that is not surprising. You would probably be surprised to know that, just as in your business, there are many other companies. In fact, in our industry, there are over 150 concerns. Ours is one of the best. Let me tell you about our company and at the same time show you our line of quality products."

The various prejudices against policies of your company and personnel are best handled by permitting prospects or customers to unburden themselves completely, and then assuring them that every effort will be made to adjust the problems that may have arisen. If the prejudice is related to you personally, and prospects indicate they do not wish to do business with you, make a strong appeal to their sense of fair play. You can say: "[Prospect's Name], I would appreciate your telling me what it is that makes you feel as you do. I would certainly like to avoid anything like this ever happening again and would be deeply indebted to you for your advice." Once the advice has been given, you can decide from the circumstances what your future opportunities are with the particular prospect or customer.

7. *Reciprocity competition.*

All sales professionals, whether they sell to retailers or to industrial consumers—particularly to the latter—will at some time be faced with reciprocity competition. This situation is typified by the buyer who says, "I buy from them because they buy from us." Carefully handled, this objection frequently can be removed and can save many a sale that seemed lost at the outset. To answer this objection, you must convince prospects that in buying from you they will not lose the reciprocating customer. This can be done while emphasizing the value aspect of your proposition. Point out the numerous benefits to be gained by use of your product or service, and apply the "Yes-But" technique: "[Prospect's Name], I certainly can understand how you feel. There isn't anyone in business who wouldn't do everything to keep his customers. None of us wants to lose a single one of them. The farthest thing from my mind is to do anything that might cause you to offend yours. If you pause to think the situation over, you'll see there is really no reason not to give me this order now, and the next to your customer. I say this because, as I have shown, you stand to profit a great deal with our line of merchandise and the excellent service we offer. Not only that, you are assured of two splendid sources instead of one—a guarantee of interruption-free operations." Here, you have given your prospects an opportunity to use their powers of reasoning to justify their decision to give you the order. If you use the method recommended, you need not find this type of objection as frustrating as it would seem.

Two Suggestions

1. *Never knock your competitors!* To do so is to give publicity to your competitors and to raise doubt in your prospects' minds. They will say to themselves, "I had better take a look at the line of this sales professional's competitor. Why would it be selling so well if it were obviously no good?" The result is often a lost order. Always remember: If you constantly attack your competitors, your prospect may feel called on to defend them, out of a sense of fair play. When the prospect or customer brings up the question of competition, it is better to say, "There is no question that that company makes a fine product. To be truthful, there isn't a single manufacturer in this industry that doesn't. The reason that I joined [Your Company's Name] is that I firmly believed that it had the finest products of them all. Feature for feature, I can prove this to you." The sales professional then starts to develop the facts and evidence. Note carefully that the sales professional mentions the competition—but not by name. Creative sales professionals never make unpleasant or unkind remarks about their competitors; they rely on their ability as sales professionals, and on the product they have to offer, when competition is brought into the picture. They emphasize the superior points of their own product and waste no derogatory words on the competition. You will have few sales without meeting some form of competition, but it is always foolish to heap abuse on your competitors and to speak disparagingly about their products. No one expects a sales professional to ignore competition. This would hardly be realistic. You will be expected to meet it on the grounds suggested: in terms of the superior features, value, and quality that your proposition represents.

2. *Project your loyalty to the company you serve.* Too often, sales professionals may agree with a customer, in an effort to smooth away objections, and may then proceed to make even worse criticisms of their own company. They can make no worse error. Every negative remark sales professionals make about the house they represent results in loss of respect for themselves, their company, and their products or services. Recognize that every individual respects the quality of loyalty in people. If you can no longer maintain loyalty, change your position.

Quick Tips on Handling Objections

As you prepare for a presentation:

- ✓ Be sure you are addressing the decision maker(s).
- ✓ Be certain that nothing can cause the appointment to be postponed.

✓ Be sure that you have discussed all relevant financial and budget factors before you begin.

✓ Be sure you have a grasp of your prospect's goals and desires and of any problem(s) that threaten their realization. Move the prospect toward a desire to solve the problem.

✓ Demonstrate that your products provide a preferred solution.

As objections surface:

✓ *Never argue.* Don't ever respond to an objection by arguing with the prospect. An argument can easily be perceived as sales pressure. Instead of jumping at a chance to win a debate, use the objection as an opportunity to learn more.

✓ *Never attack.* Distinguish between the prospect and the objection. You want to overcome the objection, not the prospect. Try to sense what your prospect is really feeling, and show genuine concern for your prospect without any implication that you are out to prove him or her wrong. Such an implication can become a personal attack that can threaten a prospect's self-esteem.

✓ *Listen carefully.* Always let the prospect state his or her objection without interruption. Be sure that you understand what the prospect is trying to communicate. Convey that you respect the prospect and that you think the prospect's opinions are important.

✓ *Use "and," not "but."* When you encounter an objection, try not to use the word "but." Use "and" instead. A prospect who hears "but" may feel challenged or rejected. Your prospect will be more likely to listen if you use "and."

✓ *Restate the objection.* This will often lead a prospect to answer his or her own objection. Introduce your paraphrasing by saying: "Let's see if I understand you correctly. You said. . . ." The prospect will readily clarify anything you may have missed, and will see your attempt as evidence of genuine concern.

✓ *Invite elaboration.* Ask your clients to elaborate on their objection. This should be done with an attitude of sincerity and concern, not with sarcasm or contempt. This approach often results in a motivation to resolve the objection themselves, and it buys you some time as you attempt to classify the objection and prepare to close the sale.

✓ *Respond positively.* Respond in a way that conveys care for the prospect: "I'm glad you brought that up. Many people felt the same way you do until they learned [your response]."

✓ *Reinforce your attitude nonverbally.* Maintain eye contact, maintain a nonthreatening posture, and speak calmly.

✓ *Confirm your effective response.* Be sure that the prospect has bought into your response the objections. *Don't assume* that he or she has. Use phrases like "That clarifies that point quite well, doesn't it?" or "That's the answer you are looking for, isn't it?" or "With that question out of the way, we can go ahead, don't you think?"

✓ *Move on!* Once you have the prospect's agreement that the objection is no longer a problem, proceed to the next step in the sales process. Do not dwell on the topic.

Objections Determine Objectives

One of the keys to effective handling of objections is sensitivity—especially when listening to the prospect. How do most arguments perpetuate themselves? One party starts shouting, then the other shouts, and the volume and intensity accelerate. In contrast, when one person whispers or talks low and slow, the other party does the same. When a child cries, degrees, volume, speed, goals, and objectives are communicated. The child learns early that different cries will bring different responses. Children can gain their parents' various communications, even before the younger generation can speak. Adult humans do not articulate by words alone. Body language counts.

For there to be communication, there have to be three elements: (1) a message, (2) a sender, and (3) a receiver. The tallest tree in the forest can fall and make the loudest noise of the year, but if no one hears it, what's the impact? Nothing. When a baby cries and no one reacts, the infant will vary the pace and pitch, depending on the severity of the need—being wet, cold, hungry, in pain, or bored. The crying may even stop.

When older children misbehave and we have to guide and train them, we must use our craft in reacting so that we convey we have received the message and we are responding. As an example, when sibling rivalry arises and one sibling hits the other, there are a number of ways to respond. If you want a full-blown argument and denial session, say something along the following line: "You are a bad boy to be hitting your sister. Keep it up and you're going to get some of your own treatment." If you want to use this event, which you know will recur in the future, as a training lesson and still not have your kid hate you temporarily, consider this alternative, "Hitting is a dangerous thing. Sister could really get hurt. Let's talk about it. What happened to make you that angry?"

A couple of things went on here. In the first instance, the child was assailed and a threat was made. In the second, the event, rather than the individual, was the focus of the discussion, and a question was asked.

I saw that! Come into a roomful of fighting kids, calm them down, and then ask what went on here, and they will all say, "Nothing." Says one MDRT sales professional,

> When my kids were youngsters and I came home, the first thing I did on walking into a room was say, "I saw that." Then, it was tough to turn off the flow and I had to listen as fast as I could to get caught up on the day's details. Everyone squealed on everyone else. I couldn't believe everything I heard, but I quickly got a picture of the whole day's activities. I didn't want to be a referee, so I didn't take any action. I only listened and said, "Oh." By asking rather than accusing, I instantly made communication and was part of the dialogue.
>
> Even though I didn't directly ask a question, it was a question anyway. They wondered what did I see and immediately thought of events in which they were not involved, individually. They were defending themselves but they were also listening to what their sisters were saying and I didn't take too much of it seriously but I was made current. In addition, it started a dialogue for the evening.

Have you ever seen someone railing at a television set because of disagreement with what was being said? The comments were addressed to a person who wasn't even present or who may have been starring in a film that was made years before. However, the verbalizing establishes the link of a dialogue rather than a monologue. It verifies a sender, a receiver, and a message. Salespeople must first get the attention of their listeners, who will then object, or agree, or get intensely absorbed with dialogue. Until the dialogue begins, there is only a sentiment of courtesy because the meeting was requested, or even an attitude of "Show me."

Every interview consists of two parts: (1) the tension part and (2) the task part. Every sales meeting has a tension segment while the two factions paw for territory. Even friendly animals circle each other until they are sure of the atmosphere. Your selling is most effective when a need is firmly established and understood, but you may never get that far if there is still doubt and chill in your customer's speculations. Sometimes, the tension part is only 10 seconds, and sometimes it is much longer. It may not go away during the whole interview. One thing is certain: If it isn't abated, there will not be a sale.

Therefore, a little talk about the weather or about sports or the accoutrements of the office (or other meeting location) is a good thing. It relieves the tension. Conversely, too much of it detracts from the aim of the gathering. Until the tension is softened, there is no sense going on with the task part. The listener's mind is not opened. If all the approaching and groundwork have been done properly, this segment should not last too long. After all, prospects know why you are there, and they do have a tinge of curiosity. After a few minutes of pleasant small talk, people start becoming familiar and comfortable with each other. Sales foreplay is important to the total process.

Most of what goes on is your attitude. Both parties to a transaction are usually on the same wavelength, but in a sales situation the participants take sides until a common covenant is reached. The early attitude determines what goes on throughout. In short, rely on yourself to accomplish most of what you do in life. If you get assistance from your correspondents, everything will go smoother, but the old adage about doing things yourself is especially true in sales.

The agenda for any meeting should be set by you, since you called and asked for the appointment. Therefore, do thorough preplanning for what will take place in the conference. The attorneys in a criminal trial rarely ask a question to which they do not already know the answer. Your best sales situations are those in which you are familiar with the presentations and with the people. Study and constant groundwork are essential. The will to win means nothing without the will to prepare.

Remember those early prepared presentations you had to learn in the company training program—the ones you thought were hokey? Be honest and admit how frequently you fall back on them and use all or parts of them.

Every time two people meet, one (or both) of them is selling something. In dealing with tradespeople, your goal may be to get something done—more importantly, to get it done with the least amount of agony and upset for yourself. You expect the worst. You try to steer the transactions so that you get what you want without verbal or mental confrontations. As one MDRT sales professional points out:

> My wife and I travel a lot, with much baggage and material. I used to get comments from the bellhop and cab drivers about how heavy the stuff was, or was it all ours? Now, we have gotten rid of all the sarcasm and questioning by reversing the roles and doing to them what they used to do to us. We still travel heavy, but now I am the one to say, "It's heavy. Can you handle it?" The typical reaction from the server is a macho one. He or she thinks internally, "Of course I can handle it!" My question also conveys confidence in the fact that I am aware of what I have, and if the situation is not right, someone else can handle it. The usual quick response is "Yep," and they then have to live by their word.

If you approach the support staff in your office with an attitude of, "This will be tough but I know you can handle it," they will back off as soon as it does get a little heavy, and they'll come back to you for help or some form of easement. Yet, a slightly different approach, using almost the same words, will bring grossly different results. Try saying: "This will not be difficult. Go as far as you can." This allows the person to experiment and go forward freely, not knowing what his or her outer limit is, yet knowing you are available when needed, because you did not mention a negative or tightly defined target. It usually works well in expanding someone's horizons and overcoming a need for constant reaffirmation.

You can control most of what goes on in an interview by saying the right words early and moderating what transpires as the meeting evolves. You can transmit a message that what is happening is formidable and negative, or you can indicate it is logical and comfortable. You know there are going to be objections and questions, but you can help them to be reasonable and aspiring rather than confrontational and challenging. No sales professional would start an interview by saying (using a life insurance sales situation as an example), "This is deep subject matter, and you have to die to get the benefit for your beneficiaries." The client's mind would shut like a bear trap, and the rest of the appointment would be polite indifference or wriggly abiding until the client could get you out of there.

However, if you greet your prospects with an attitude of, "Come, let us reason together," a whole different stage is set. Consider even the earliest contact you have with your prospects— making the first appointment. Which of these phrases do you think would make more headway? "Can I see you on Monday or Wednesday?" or "Can you see me on Monday or Wednesday?" In the first instance, the sales professional is the subject and the client is the object. There was a choice of days, but the client was not given even a hint of a chance of arranging the appointment. Only a preposition changed in the second question, but the client suddenly was put in the place of the decision maker. He or she was the subject rather than the object. He or she had options. This takes away the feeling of being led.

The two questions above are examples of giving choices and of using the right words so as not to veer toward an objection if none is apparent. Let's take the same theme, making appointments. How can you get rid of the initial objection to having the meeting in the first place and, at the same time, make it potentially more profitable to you? Try this question: "When can you come in?" The prospect stays in the director's chair, but you're now alongside in the chief's chair.

This question does a number of things for you, but it is still a fatal alternative. Rather than giving a choice of two, either one of which would result in a favorable situation for you, it introduced one word that has the same effect. "When" gives innumerable choices that are in the prospect's mind, not in yours. However, the bonus comes from the assumption that there will be a meeting, and it will be in your office. Think of all the positives of having the appointment in your home territory.

Just the fact that you ask the question indicates to the prospect that you expect to have the meeting in your office. Your confidence in suggesting the meeting in your office states that you are in control, and this is normal procedure for you. People will react as you expect them to react. People expect sales professionals to have confidence—in their emotions and their products. It is not pushy and it is not excessively assertive to lead the sales process in the most efficient fashion. It is a benefit to both parties.

The prospect now knows the subject of the entire discussion, because the meeting will be in an office, without outside distractions. You can save lots of time and certainly lots of expense and wear on your automobile. If a question arises that needs research, you can do it right then, as opposed to having a loose end that might necessitate another meeting. The focus is on the subject *you* present. You are in control. You also appear more professional.

A prospect who is not used to coming to a sales office will mildly object to doing so. Here's a pretty effective response: "Sometimes, you can make more money planning than you can by making more money." Another is: "Sometimes, you can save more time planning than you can by not focusing. I promise you: No distractions. And probably less time spent, overall, than if we had met any other place."

Try a few on-site meetings and see whether the activity coming into your office picks up. This is a great method of overcoming a lot of objections. When prospects come to your site, they exhibit a sizable element of trust; you can focus on what's important and eliminate some of the excess fluff.

Words Alone Don't Tell the Whole Story

When you speak to prospects on the phone, and you can only hear their voices, can you tell what their mood is? Suppose they are saying all the right words. Nothing untoward is being uttered. Can you determine whether they are tight-lipped? Can you sense a strain, even over the wires? The words are crisp and cold. There is an edge to the conversation. There is no warmth and no added glee in the dialogue; in fact, it is not even a dialogue. Both parties may be talking but only one is conversing. You're in a monologue connected by phone wires.

Conversely, can you determine when someone is especially happy on the other end of the phone? You can hear the smiles even though you can't see them. This is not even body language. This is just ear language. You are functioning like a blind person, who can hear infinitely more sounds than a sighted person.

Sight, Sound, Touch, Smell, Taste

You are endowed with these five senses if you are fortunate enough to be healthy. Jokingly and flippantly, we talk about people who have a sixth sense. As a sales professional, you should have that other sense of *what is really going on*—all of the above plus a vital sense for sales professionals: awareness. Your process of filtering objections can be made much simpler if you apply all of your senses to what your prospects are saying and what their body language is telling you.

Commonly, a prospect's third objection is the real one, but all of them are important. Show your complete attention by listening to them and legitimately indicating you are taking this whole appointment seriously. You must acknowledge everything that takes place in an interview. If you slight some part of it and it appears the client has not noticed or accepts the short version, time will indicate this is not the case. When you tramp on a blade of grass, it stays down for a while but then it pops up again. Conscious, subconscious, and innate feelings all get recorded and come out in time.

Everything in the setting is consequential to the gathering. Doing the appointment in your office is best, but even in the home of the prospect, you should be the one to take charge. If the table in the living room is not suitable to the meeting, you can easily and comfortably gain control and positive influence by asking for slight changes. For instance, if there is a radio playing while you are talking, do not try to talk over it or ignore it. Ask if it is all right to turn it down. Invariably, the other party will say, "Why don't I turn it off?" You get the effect you want, and you gain a little control. You have done it in an unobtrusive way, but your listener will now listen to you.

If a table is messy and you need some room, don't shove all the stuff aside. Ask if it's okay to move whatever it is you want moved.

This shows respect for the property of others but lets them know you are aware of what is going on around you. It also states that this is a formal meeting and certain decorum is to be followed. Probably, they will move the stuff themselves. In any event, all eyes and ears will be on you. When the prospects see that you are in your jurisdiction, even in their domain, the objections will be fewer.

If you see another part of the area that would be convenient and better for the interview, ask if it is okay to move over. Then stand up and start walking in that direction. This will, again, show you are serious about the meeting, and you intend to put it into the best possible aura.

Saying Isn't Always Meaning

Sometimes, an objection is only words that are mouthed. Body language will tell you the seriousness of the intent. Remember, most objections are only conversation. It is good when *something* is said, rather than nothing. When the old plaint, "I can't afford it" comes, most of the time it isn't true. However, it should never be a surprise. It is probably the objection we hear the most. It is a knee-jerk reaction on the part of the customer. Most often, it is just a way of saying, "Tell me more."

You should be able to handle this response by asking additional questions or repeating the highlights you wish to emphasize. On the other hand, if the prospect stands up and screams, "I can't afford it!" the body language says more than the words. You would tend to believe this person, and you might suggest that some other time would be better to discuss your product or service. Then you have the option to call back or not.

If the prospect tries to put the meeting off until a later date, this is invoking the "Postponable" aspect. Once again, he or she is saying, "Tell me more. I hear what you are saying, but I have not heard enough yet to make me take immediate action."

If the prospect loosens up and smiles, joins in the conversation, gives honest answers, and emanates an atmosphere of friendliness, that body language is also revealing. It indicates an open environment of sincere exchange. This atmosphere makes it enjoyable to do what we should be doing in every interview: exposing a need properly so that the solution is sorely coveted.

One Step Ahead: Anticipate the Objection

Sales professionals can develop powerful skills by learning to anticipate objections. When sales professionals thoroughly understand their prospects' needs and attitudes, they should be able to evaluate their prospects' true concerns.

The sales process should remain predictable. Sales professionals will use a fact-finder to determine needs, design a solution model, present the model, and close the sale. Sales professionals who anticipate objections facilitate the process of understanding (1) their prospects' questions and concerns, and (2) how the model resolves these questions and concerns.

Prospects will say either that they don't need your products or services, or they don't want to spend that much money on them. Prospects may say they want to wait, or they want to look at other alternatives. Regardless of what prospects say, sales professionals should be prepared and have a good answer.

Let's say that a prospect is employed in a good size company. The sales professional knows that the prospect has a lot of respect for his or her peers. If there is a suspicion that the prospect will want to discuss the proposal with a peer, the sales professional should consider offering to meet with the peer and go over the proposal, before the prospect can express any concern. This enables the sales professional to turn a potential negative into a positive opportunity.

There is a rule that says: You don't have a potential sale until you have a problem. Sales professionals should anticipate problems. After problems have surfaced, sales professionals have a chance to resolve them satisfactorily and make clients out of their prospects.

Prospects may signal their unreadiness to make a decision by hesitating or procrastinating. By forcing prospects to move too quickly, sales professionals run the risk of ruining the relationship. By showing understanding and compassion, sales professionals signal a true concern for their prospects' needs—and strengthen the bond of trust between them and their prospects.

If prospects say, "I want to wait," sales professionals need to review their prospects' objectives and reconfirm their understanding of their prospects' goals. Sales professionals could say, "I heard you say that you want to wait. Would you mind if I asked you a question? Will waiting make this decision any easier for you? All waiting does is make it harder and more expensive to accomplish your objectives."

By anticipating objections, sales professionals put themselves on the offensive instead of waiting for the objection that puts them on the defensive. Many trainers will reach a strategy often referred to as the three Rs: repeat, reassure, and resume. A recommended approach is to penetrate and precipitate action. Sales professionals need to learn to say things like, "I sense that you . . . ," "I believe, like you . . . ," or "If I were in your shoes. . . ." If sales professionals say the objection first, then prospects cannot take ownership of the problem. If prospects say them first, they can claim ownership and then defend the objection.

Ask Questions

Often, there are objections because the fact finding has not developed a strong enough need. If the prospect doesn't feel a need, then the chances of making a sale are not good. The sales professional must establish a need. If this is done, most objections fall by the wayside.

One of the ways to establish a need is to ask questions during the first interview, any time prior to the close in a one-interview sale situation. For example, you could ask prospects why they recently made a large purchase, or why they are interested in the products you sell. Their answers may provide clues to what motivates them and how you can position your products in front of them. It becomes difficult, later on in the close, for prospects to say they don't need your products or services. You already know what motivates them.

Record Answers

Be sure to conduct a very thorough fact-finding phase, during which you ask prospects to share their most important personal and financial goals. Be sure to record this information. During the close, it can be used effectively to diffuse certain objections.

PROSPECT: "I would love to do this, but since we last talked some new expenses have arisen, and I cannot afford to purchase your product now. Let's get together on this later."

SALES PROFESSIONAL: ". . . for instance—what expenses?"

PROSPECT: "Uh . . . new tires and a vacation."

SALES PROFESSIONAL: "I can surely understand. Expenses will always arise. But let's review the personal financial and family/business goals you shared with me the last time we visited, and make sure that I have them recorded correctly. Let me see, you said that financial stability and your family/business ability to remain in its own world were your greatest concerns. However, if I am hearing you correctly, I should change this part here to read 'tires and vacations.' Is this correct?"

PROSPECT: "Uh. . . ."

SALES PROFESSIONAL: "Wouldn't it be possible for you to have tires and also purchase what I am proposing?"

Overcome Fears and Program Your Brain to Sell

MDRT represents the elite of the financial services industry worldwide. Yet, amazingly, nine out of ten of its members have mild restrictive fears; one out of ten has severe restrictive fears—phobias, or things they don't like to do or can't do; and one out of twenty of its members has intrusive obsessive thoughts or rituals that can't be overcome. In fact, the more intelligent, creative, and imaginative MDRT members are, the more likely they are to have fear!

Thus, most sales professionals have a bag full of worries and fears. Some have a small bag and some have a large bag. Perhaps you have a gunnysack full. Let's examine how your bag gets filled, and, more important, how to empty it.

Normal human beings have fears; normal human beings have psychological problems; normal human beings have phobias and obsessions, and it's okay. The problem is that when they are left unchallenged, these fears limit and constrict sales professionals at every level of human endeavor.

Why have a fear mechanism? The body has a system to deal with dire emergencies, the so-called "fight-or-flight mechanism." You have, on the top of your kidneys, two small glands that secrete the most powerful stimulating drug in your body—adrenaline. When it is released, blood surges into your muscles, doubling or quadrupling your strength. You are ready to kill a lion bare-handed. You have read stories of a 70-year-old grand-mother who goes out in the backyard and sees her grandson trapped under a car that has slipped off a jack. She runs over and lifts the car off him. The next day, someone calculates the force necessary to lift the car as 700 pounds, but the grand-mother, in a nonemergency setting, can generate only 100 pounds. That extra 600 pounds came from adrenaline. A great drug for killing lions and lifting cars, but not very good when you're trying to make a sales presentation, give a talk, or make a cold call.

Brain in the Bag

Do you know the world's record for "brain jumping?" Did you see the most recent Olympic Games? That wasn't a medal event. Brains don't jump; they have no legs. Your brain acts as if it is lying behind a six-foot wall. It only knows what's going on by what you tell it.

The brain believes everything you tell it. It cannot distinguish real from imagined. The brain is a high-speed computer. It makes 100 million computations per second and cannot be wrong. If you program a computer to calculate $2 + 2 = 5$, it will take that for fact and will not correct itself.

From the moment a human is born, the empty brain begins to program itself. Unfortunately, in our harsh competitive and com-parative society, many of our early programs are quite negative. Destructive put-downs by parents, friends, peers, and authority figures go into your bag!

Negative Programs

It has been estimated that by the time you have reached age 18, you will have heard 180,000 negative personal comments and

25,000 hours of negative authoritarian input. Thus, most of the beliefs in your "bag" are negative and failure messages. Fifty percent of the brain programs that you have were placed in your brain by age five. Eighty percent of the programs were placed there by age eight. Thus, most of the decisions about your life are being made by an eight-year-old kid whom you may not even like. Would you seek personal, vocational, or financial advice from an eight-year-old guru? Of course not!

Disneyland

Do you know what happens to four-year-olds in Disneyland? They spend the whole day banging into adults' knees and thighs. To a four-year-old, an adult is a 17-foot, 800-pound giant blocking out the sun! Down from those towering heights come a booming, authoritative voice replete with put-downs. Those are the messages that program your early brain.

As a child, you accept whatever you hear, and because you don't challenge those programs, they remain like posthypnotic suggestions that control your every action. Now, add some guilt messages about wasting your time, being immature, spending too much time playing, or not settling down, and the bag becomes a little heavier. Finally, mix in a liberal sprinkling of failure messages and rejection, and your bag is bulging.

Brain Priorities

The only two things that the brain doesn't do are: die or be demeaned. If, at any time, your brain believes that your life is threatened or your ego may be challenged, large amounts of adrenaline will be released and you will experience classic anxiety symptoms.

The two most common phobias are:

1. Fear of public speaking.

2. Fear of death.

Given the order of the phobias' importance, this means most people would rather die than give a speech; they are concerned about making a mistake or being critically judged. Comedians express that concern: If you do poorly as a comic, you "die" or "bomb." If you do well, you "slay" or "kill" your audience. The language describes the threat of the event.

What most people don't realize is that selling is often a speaking engagement before an audience of one! Many social interactions are, again, dealing with audiences of one! Some people can give a speech to an audience of 1,000 people without fear, and those same people can't get up the courage to make a cold call or a sales presentation, or ask someone out for a date, without significant anxiety. It all depends on what your "brain in the bag" is saying to you.

If your brain says your prospect might reject you, and you might lose the sale that could ruin your reputation, and so on—every word causes your body to release adrenaline. When you use scare words, you shake your bag. Every shake is associated with a release of that most powerful drug, and you might feel symptoms such as shortness of breath, sweating, rapid heart rate, chest tightness—impending doom! Every negative statement is attended by a large squirt of adrenaline: "I will get rejected" . . . "I will be ridiculed by my peers" . . . "My wife (or husband) will think less of me" . . . "I'll lose my job" . . . "If I don't reach my sales quota, I'll be demoted."

As you continue to release more and more adrenaline because of scary thoughts running wild, you experience even more discomforting symptoms. You may have difficulty concentrating or remembering, or a feeling of unreality and a tremendous urge to flee the situation. Your fear has become unmanageable. You simply avoid the activity to avoid the pain. You procrastinate. You freeze. Watch your mouth—your brain is listening!

The "What Ifs" and the WPTs

As you continue to mature, you fill your bag with two common childhood fears that persist into adulthood: the "what ifs" and the "WPTs." The what ifs are imagined disasters: What if there's a monster in the closet? What if I screw up? What if they see I'm nervous, incompetent, shivering, quivering? You continue to imagine catastrophic events in selling and social situations.

The WPTs are "What People Think." What will people think if they see a spot on my tie? What will people think if they know that underneath this calm face is a quaking, frightened human being? In your desperate desire to be liked and accepted, you place tremendous value on what others think about you.

Your bag is filled with "what ifs" and "WPTs," and you will hear them clearly in challenging new endeavors.

Your Sentry

Finally, you adopt a protective sentry to sit on your shoulder—on guard 24 hours a day—to ensure the safety of your life and your precious ego. That sentry's voice limits your escalation to higher goals because it knows your limitations and it doesn't want you to fail. That voice limits exploration because you might get rejected or perhaps even fired. That voice must be recognized and challenged if you are to grow. It reminds you of "what ifs" and "WPTs," your deficits, your weaknesses, your guilt and failures—all in an incessant and limiting babble.

Most sales professionals are so used to that negative voice that they are rarely conscious of its presence. It controls them, but they don't hear it.

170 Million Addicts

If you think this is an exaggeration of the effects of carrying a negative bag, consider this: It is estimated that 170 million people in the United States are addicted to drugs, alcohol, work, cigarettes, and/or food. Populationwise, there are 170 million adults in the United States. Thus, if one defines an addiction as a destructive habit that eases the pain we feel as incomplete human beings, it means that virtually every adult in our society at one time has had, or currently is embracing, a destructive addiction, an obsessive desire to do something to calm that frightened eight-year-old that still lives with the adult exterior.

It is imperative that you understand the consequences of allowing your bags to go unchallenged. If you don't understand what's in your bag, you may always feel like an impostor, regardless of the level of your success. Failure is easy; you're programmed well for that. But success is different. Success carries expectations, success demands increasing responsibilities and performance. Success is scary.

Don't be too discouraged; in reality, everyone carries that loathsome bag into adulthood. The goal is to spring-clean it and lighten it. You start by recognizing the contents of your bag. Tune in to the messages. What are they saying? Whose voice is it? Is it helping you? Once you hear and accept the messages, you can do something about them.

Thought Stoppage

The most powerful tool for challenging destructive or scary messages is a process called thought stoppage. By carefully monitoring your internal voice, you can begin to scrutinize every inaccurate, limiting, or failure-oriented message. You do this by saying "Stop," taking a deep breath, and counting to four slowly. The word "stop" is like a computer message informing your brain that the last statement was unacceptable and the brain will now be reprogrammed. From now on, any unacceptable message must be stopped immediately. Following the fourth count, you dispute the accuracy of the prior statement and then change or reframe it, making it a positive supporting message.

This method can be used in any life situation, but particularly when you are embarking on new and challenging endeavors and the failure voices are very loud. Use thought stoppage immediately every time, and you will clean up a lot of restricting mental programs.

Fear

"FEAR" stands for:

F = False

E = Exaggerations

A = Appearing

R = Real

Much of that sentry voice you hear is exaggerated and inaccurate, and it causes unnecessary alarm with its consequent secretion of adrenaline. The phrase "dying of embarrassment" exemplifies this. You don't die from being embarrassed, but that phrase will shake your bag because it is a "false exaggeration appearing real." To stop scaring yourself, you must begin to listen very carefully to what you say to yourself in any stressful situation. If it's negative, destructive, or exaggerated, use your thought stoppage. Challenge the accuracy. Was it a fact or an imagined catastrophe? Ask yourself: "What am I saying to myself? Is it helpful?"

From now on, challenge and dispute every negative statement you hear: "If I ask for a commitment, the customer won't give it to me." Dispute: "That's not a fact, that's a belief, and beliefs are often false." Reframe: "If I get commitment, the customer will feel relieved at not having to see any more salespeople." Inner statement: "There's a recession. If I ask for a larger order, they'll probably turn me down!" Stop! "1, 2, 3, 4." Dispute: "That's not a fact, that's a belief, and beliefs are frequently untrue." Reframe: "I'll ask and give them a chance to answer. If I don't ask, my failure rate will be 100 percent." Inner statement: "I think they think I'm pushing too hard." Stop! "1, 2, 3, 4." Dispute: "I don't know that for a fact." Reframe: "I'll just have to risk being as assertive as I choose." And, finally, for you travelers: Inner statement: "Airplanes are unsafe." Stop! "1, 2, 3, 4." Dispute: "They are the safest form of transportation. You would have to fly every single day for 26,000 years to be on a plane that crashes." Reframe: "I won't buy a ticket on any plane that's going to crash."

From now on, challenge every statement, and dispute and reframe it. Excellent examples of disputing and reframing can be found in a sales script book. Do you own one? Intriguingly, it gives you clues to countering everyday sales situations, but it also is a marvelous guide to reframing your own internal thoughts. When you hear one of your negative statements, create a number of personal scripts that dispute and, thus, empower you.

Updating Your Sentry

Sentries in the front lines are often deprived of incoming information. The tools you use to reprogram your brain and your sentry are victories. The brain doesn't believe what you say—it pays attention only to accomplishments. Thus, after disputing and re-framing, reel off the victories you have made. Tell your brain about your prowess; reassure and calm it by relating the growth and changes you have made. Don't let an eight-year-old contaminate your adult decisions. Challenge and reframe. Use thought stoppage immediately, every time!

Success Tools

To improve your selling success, you need intimate awareness of your bag contents. Challenge all negative nicknames or labels—they are limiting and invariably false. Dispute them and replace them with positive affirmations—positive statements about yourself. Don't let unimportant grammar-school experiences limit you in adult life. All people lack social skills and confidence as youths, but unless you challenge your fears as an adult, they will persist. All reluctance is invariably associated with childhood fears of rejection and failure. Dispute and reframe: "A rejection of a request is not a rejection of me." "What if they don't like me?" Dispute and reframe: "Not everybody has to like me. I only have to please myself."

Eight-year-olds have a desperate need to be liked, to be popular, and to be accepted. As they mature, they realize that these are not adult goals. Unless we change those early programs, we will continue to seek gratification outside of ourselves, and we will be extremely vulnerable to feelings of failure and rejection.

Disneyland Revisited

Remember that Disneyland visit? The 800-pound, 17-foot giants? Did you know at age four that you would be this big? Own your own car? Have your own credit card? Be an aspiring or successful sales professional? Of course not! Tell your sentry you're the giant now—you can spring-clean your bag of negativity and replace it with mature, supporting, nurturing success messages.

Be aware that escalation to any higher level will release a torrent of negative failure programs from your bag. To grow, you must hear those messages and dispute and reframe every one of them. Your sentry knows your level of comfort. It tolerates gradual growth but becomes alarmed at dramatic changes. It will warn you with large releases of adrenaline, and the subsequent feelings of discomfort may discourage you from trying. Learn to reassure that frightened sentry.

Perceived Efficaciousness

Confidence develops from your belief that you can effectively handle a situation (perceived efficaciousness). The more confident you are of a successful outcome, the less your discomfort. Tell your bag, "I can handle it!" Remember, growth depends on successful endeavors—victories. The brain doesn't believe words. It only believes victories. Keep track, and faithfully record every successful endeavor. Reviewing those victories will create a growth mentality and allow you to ascend to higher and higher success levels.

Asking

Often, you don't ask for something because you are afraid of being rejected. As a child, if you asked for something and you didn't get it, you felt unloved. "If they loved me, they would have given it to me." Your sentry often reminds you of that sequence and makes it difficult for you to ask for things.

However, if you don't ask, your failure rate is 100 percent. You can ask for anything! Now you know: No one can reject *you*—they can only reject your request.

Most people have difficulty saying "No." As a child, if you said "No" to a parent or authority figure, you were liable to be punished. Asking forces people to deal with the difficulty of saying "No." Quench that childhood fear. Stifle your sentry and ask, ask, ask!

Desensitization

Overcoming call reluctance invariably deals with failure and rejection messages—the "what ifs" and the "WPTs." The "brain in the bag" does not recognize the difference between real and imagined, so you can practice call and sales situations with peers and friends. Set up the imagined situations, let your support group reject and harass you and say everything you don't want to hear. Practice dealing with those responses. You'll develop the confidence needed to handle real situations because this process desensitizes fears. Familiarity doesn't always breed contempt. Practice, practice, practice. Face your fears and they will disappear.

You can use this same technique to notch your practice up to a higher level. Your inner voice knows your level. Imagined practice sessions can rapidly escalate you to a higher level and desensitize you to the hazards at that higher, previously uncomfortable level.

Happy

Although the Declaration of Independence entitles you to the pursuit of happiness, the contents of your bag do not. "That's enough fun, put your tops away." "Idle hands are a devil's workshop." "When are you going to grow up?" This is a hurry-up society. It races us through childhood.

A four-year-old smiles 325 times a day—an adult's daily output is 15. Smiles have been beaten, scared, cynically rejected, and matured out of you. Challenge your bag, reprogram your life for pleasure time, and deal with the guilt that creates. Your goal must be to get those 310 laughs back.

Most of your limitations are created by self-perceived fears. Silence your negative sentry. Dispute and reframe your negative beliefs and failure messages. Use thought stoppage, challenge guilt programs, use your victory rehearsals to reprogram your brain, continually challenge and spring-clean your bag. Have some fun. You are the giant now.

Finding the Real Objection

A prospect's objection is frequently not real. It is most often a ploy used to say "No" without hurting a sales professional's feelings. Your first action upon encountering an objection should be to find out whether the prospect is telling the truth. Does the prospect really mean what has been said, or has a cloaking device been enlisted to get rid of you?

The technique for discovering whether an objection is real sounds something like this:

SALES PROFESSIONAL: "In your opinion, does this product make sense to you?" (Always take your prospect's temperature by asking an opinion. This is a super "trial" close because it is most likely to unveil an objection. You want the objection stated, so that you can deal with it.)

PROSPECT: "I want to think about it. . . ."

SALES PROFESSIONAL: "Obviously, you have a reason for saying that. Do you mind if I ask what it is?"

PROSPECT: "I don't mind."

SALES PROFESSIONAL: "What is it?"

PROSPECT: "I want to check out the competition."

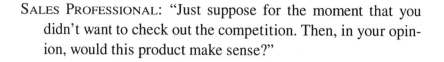

SALES PROFESSIONAL: "Just suppose for the moment that you didn't want to check out the competition. Then, in your opinion, would this product make sense?"

You asked your prospect whether the plan made sense. The prospect responded that he or she wanted to think about it, and to check out the competition. You didn't ask the prospect whether he or she wanted to think about it. You asked whether it made sense. Because the prospect responded to a question other than the one you asked, you have the right to meet his or her condition exactly and then repeat your original question.

You repeat the above line of questioning, but end it differently.

SALES PROFESSIONAL: "Just suppose for the moment that you didn't want to check out the competition. Then, in your opinion, would purchasing this product make sense?"

PROSPECT: "Well, I'm not really sure."

You have met the prospect's condition exactly, and he or she came up with another "No." The replies about wanting to think about it and checking out the competition were not real. Therefore, do not answer them. Instead, try to find out what is real.

SALES PROFESSIONAL: "Obviously, then, you must have some other reason for hesitating. Do you mind if I ask what that is?"

PROSPECT: "Money is tight right now."

SALES PROFESSIONAL: "Just suppose for the moment that money was not a problem. Then, in your opinion, would purchasing this product make sense?"

PROSPECT: "Well, I am not really sure I need it."

SALES PROFESSIONAL: "Obviously, you have some other reason for saying that. Do you mind if I ask what the real reason is?"

PROSPECT: "I don't see myself needing this."

SALES PROFESSIONAL: "Just suppose for the moment that you saw yourself needing this product. Then, in your opinion, would it make sense to purchase it?"

PROSPECT: "Well, of course, but I really don't see myself needing this immediately."

Notice that all of the objections that were not real disappeared, and the sales professional never had to answer any of them. The technique was repeated until the prospect finally admitted the true objection: The prospect cannot see himself or herself using or needing the product immediately. Now what?

SALES PROFESSIONAL: "I can understand that. Others have said that, too. But you know, that brings up a question: Will you benefit by having this product, despite your concern? Is that the question?"

The purpose here is twofold. First, as the sales professional, you want to empathize with your prospect by conveying that you understand how the prospect feels and by giving reassurance that he or she is not alone in these feelings. You do not sympathize, you empathize. Second, you use a delicate technique to change the prospect's objection into a question. By telling your prospect that a question has now been raised, and the question relates to whether there is a benefit despite his or her concern, you have changed the prospect's objection into a question. And when a prospect has a question, you have an obligation to answer it.

You cannot answer objections, but you can answer questions. The key words are, "That brings up a question: Will you benefit by having this product, despite your concern? Is that the question?" Even if your prospect says "No, that is not the question," you will win because all you have to say is "What *is* the question?" Your prospect will most likely respond by saying, "The question is . . . ," thus turning his or her own objection into a question for you. How you meet an objection is what selling is all about. If you have created the need, and your prospect has the ability to pay, you will make the sale. So if you must answer the prospect's "question," do it by reselling the need. Once you have resold the need, ask your prospect, "In your opinion, does purchasing the product now make more sense?" Then, close the sale!

Don't Mistake an Excuse for an Objection

The ability to meet an objection that is raised during the course of an interview is one of a sales professional's most valuable assets. It requires training, knowledge of product, and native intelligence. No matter how high prospects' IQs may be, or how excellent their grades were when they graduated from college, they will be at a loss to answer an objection if they do not know all the intricate facets of the material they are promoting.

"Selling is basically like every other problem," says the president of a large realty firm. "Once you can state the problem, however difficult, it can be solved." If you cannot state it, all the verbosity in the world cannot accomplish the desired result. Thus, if you can organize good answers to problems that confront prospective purchasers, or a good answer to the objections they may raise, your job is 99 percent done.

To be able to give a convincing response to an objection requires certain intellectual abilities. No two customers are going to bring forward exactly the same argument, nor will they use the same manner and words as were used by the sales trainer or manager. The same question from different customers requires a different answer or a different method of answering. To recognize the thought behind the words of the prospect and to relate this thinking to everything that you have learned over the years requires more than memory; it calls for alert intelligence.

However, one qualification is more valuable in an objection than understanding the product—if that is possible. It is the ability to differentiate between an objection and an excuse. Here is something that cannot be emphasized too strongly, for the two are as distinct as night is from day, although they have their meeting zones—their dawns and their twilights.

It is difficult to lay down a test or rule by which one can distinguish between an objection and an excuse. The difference, great though it may be, will vary both with products and with customers. In other words, an objection in one interview may be an excuse in another.

What is an objection? A top MDRT sales professional defines an objection as "an argument legitimately offered in good faith by prospects under conditions in which they are still undecided, still anxious to find the correct answer for themselves and/or their companies. They are merely uninformed or doubtful about a particular aspect of the prospective purchase."

And what is an excuse? Drawing from the same experience, and particularly from his memory of people who use excuses with abandon, this sales associate defines it as "an argument offered by prospects in an effort to seek a delay in the closing of a sale, or to avoid the closing entirely, without the unpleasant task of having to give a final 'No' to the sales professional."

From their wording, these two definitions would seem to be as unlike as an apple and an orange. But this is not true. An excuse may be offered in good faith by prospects who have deluded themselves into believing in it—and who would rise in outrage at any suggestion that it might be other than a legitimate objection.

Good sales professionals can make every objection a point to aid them in furthering the sale. Charles Brock, who many years ago, at the age of 33, became president of the largest insurance agency in the world, put it in memorable words:

> I always invite the "No's" as soon as possible in every interview. All people have a certain amount of "No's" in their system, and they have to get them out. I have always believed in asking questions early in the interview that invite a "No." As soon as I get my "No," I apply the greatest sales word I know of: *why.*
>
> Through a series of maneuvers such as this, customers sell themselves once they say "No" in their attempt to explain why they won't buy. To me, the "Yes" is the wine in the bottle. The "No" is the cork. The wine cannot be enjoyed until the cork is removed.

An objection is a valid request for further information, and it is difficult to conceive of a sale pursued from beginning to end without encountering some such requests. "I think it is quite expensive—don't you have anything cheaper?" is just such an objection. It can be met in two ways: either by finding a similar product (or plan or service, as the case may be) that is less expensive, or by demonstrating that what you are selling only seems to be expensive, but will actually cost less when one considers how great are the benefits, how long they will last, and how high is the value per dollar expended.

Yet that same statement, "I think it is too expensive," may be just an excuse, a gentle way of giving a negative answer. "We can't afford anything like this," the prospect will go on to say. Such clients may actually be well able to afford the product. The question of cost may have been reviewed time and time again during this and previous interviews, but now that they are unwilling to proceed with the closing, they are searching for an exit that will not make them appear foolish in the eyes of the sales professional or their own colleagues.

To attempt to lay down a single rule of thumb by which one can reestablish the legitimacy of a question, the good faith with which it is raised, would be impossible. Nor can sales professionals trust their own intuition. Primarily, they must rely on their knowledge of the field, their understanding of the customer, and their accumulated experience from years of selling a product. Sales professionals who recognize a request for information or an expression of doubt as nothing more than an excuse for not embarking on a course of action can and must treat the matter quite differently than they would were they to realize that such further information is legitimately required before a responsible buyer can proceed.

One MDRT associate narrated:

I recall sitting in the office of a bank president with whom I had gone over my product in minute detail. Each time, he had found another reason for not going along with it at just that moment. Patiently, I had answered each argument. Three times, my office had revised the plan, all of which meant new computations, new research, more time expended by several members of the staff. And now I was confronted by a sweet, smiling, affable gentleman who said, "I have to talk this over with my wife."

Certainly I had no objections for spousal approval, but the entire history of the previous interviews, the nature of the objections I had heard and answered for weeks, and my knowledge of how this banker functioned and how little interest his wife took in his banking affairs—all this enabled me to grasp, in a moment, a situation that I had long suspected. This man was looking for a way out.

"All right," I said, pretending to accept his objection on its face value, "why don't you discuss it with her. And call me when you're ready to go ahead?" And, as graciously as I could, I left him. I removed his card from the follow-up file—

a drastic step for me to take. Convinced that he would be a happier man if I did not pursue the matter further, I did not make another effort to close the sale.

The postscript to this story could almost be predicted. He called me about a year later and started to yell because I had not bothered to close the deal. But I know that if I had made one more call on this gentleman the previous year, not only would I have been wasting my time and his, but I would have been embarrassing him because he was trying in the kindest possible manner to turn me down.

"I have to talk this over with my wife," he had said, and I knew instantaneously that it was but an excuse. Yet when almost exactly the same words were used by another prospect and friend, I was just as certain that his was a legitimate reason for delay. Wherein lay the difference? The second person was considering a group policy in that he would personally obtain a considerable increase in the insurance coverage on his own life—a matter involving his immediate family. He had a company in which he held a controlling interest, and his wife personally participated in its management. Furthermore, I had known the client long enough to learn that he invariably discussed his business affairs with his wife and valued her knowledge and advice.

It would be foolish to categorize certain answers as objections and others as excuses. But sales professionals must be able to distinguish between them, or they will spend time and effort where no sale is to be made. For some people, an excuse is a gracious way to say "No." Prefer a "No" spoken bluntly and honestly, but recognize the word no matter how it is camouflaged.

Perhaps you dislike excuses as a method of saying "No." Perhaps you feel a prospect should have the integrity, the goodwill, and the courage to tell you that the decision is negative, and any sales professionals who can't take such an answer had better reorient his or her thinking or find another profession. Perhaps you feel that an excuse is not only intellectually questionable, but it is unkind in the long run because it often entails a continued effort to make a sale that will not materialize. Perhaps, furthermore, you view an excuse as misleading to sales professionals. The fact is that you can learn nothing profitable if you do not know the real reasons for failure to effectuate a given sale.

There are occasions when executives are not in a position to divulge the reasons for their negative answers. A company struggling against the specter of bankruptcy and reorganization would hardly want to tell a sales professional that impending financial disaster makes even the least expensive purchase of a given commodity or service impossible. The true financial condition of such a firm may have been so effectively concealed from the public that the sales professional is unaware of this hidden difficulty. In such a case, there should be no reason why an executive cannot say that the purchase has been definitely rejected, but he or she is unable to discuss the matter or to divulge the reasons. This is kindness, it is honesty, and it is fair play.

In reality, there is a "twilight zone" between objections and excuses. For instance, there is the use of a legitimate argument, in good faith, to stave off an action that is being demanded by the entire course of events. Everything that has been happening points to the closing, but the prospect is constantly asking for time for further reflection, to be sure that he or she is not making a mistake. There are people who are impulsive and quick to act even about the most significant decisions; others require leisurely thought before translating the desire into the deed.

People in the latter category would not resort to saying they had to talk the matter over with their spouses. All their objections are genuine. They are merely more numerous than they should be; they include the far-fetched as well as the practical. Under such circumstances, prospects toss about objections willy-nilly—all that they can think of, the real and the imaginary—in order to prop up their weakened resistance and find reasons not to act, rather than to obtain further necessary information.

Such prospects should be given their answers and then faced with an "either–or." Their delaying questions are not the safety valves of the inveterate procrastinator. Both types of queries should be legitimately answered, but in dealing with the ones that border on excuses, sales professionals should be careful not to allow themselves to be sidetracked to a tangent leading further and further away from the closing. Is the pathway of the question and answer, the conversations and the discussion, leading to a closing of the sale? That is the criterion, the test that must always be kept in the forefront. If the answer is "No," one must return to the road without delay.

Sales professionals must carry the discussion into the channels and paths that they desire, but in so doing they must allow prospective buyers to feel that *they* are actually leading the talks. Whenever possible, have the objections and excuses come up when you want them to, when you are ready for them. For example, objections on grounds of high price are most effectively met after prospects have been fully convinced of the merits of the offer and the help it can give them. Then your argument for closing will be stronger than it would have been earlier in the discussion. "Too expensive, you say? But just the contrary; this product offers more savings to your company in labor, repair, and space, than you are spending now. It is precisely because it is such an inexpensive and money-saving piece of equipment that you need it." From this point, one can go on to show how remarkable is the offer.

It's important to emphasize that everything said is applicable whenever and wherever a product is to be sold. Go behind the counter in the smallest store or the largest one and you will hear many objections and excuses that must be sifted and answered if there is to be effective selling.

Here are four guiding epigrams that can immeasurably help you in your selling endeavors:

1. There is no excuse, but there is always a reason for it.

2. There is nothing objectionable about an objection, but there may be about the answer to it.

3. Nothing is as objectionable as an excuse masquerading as an objection!

4. Let's make it an objective to meet every objection.

Cushion, Isolate, Smoke Out

When you must respond to an objection, you should first take a deep breath and relax. Then begin to cushion, isolate, and smoke out the objection. These and other special techniques are effective countering skills that you can practice before using them.

Cushion

The goal here is to make the prospect feel good about the objection without agreeing with him or her. For example, if the prospect says that he or she wants to think about closing the deal, you would say, "That's normal. Would you mind sharing with me why you feel this way?" That is the cushion.

Isolate

Make sure you won't be getting a series of more objections. "In addition to that, is there any other reason standing in your way?" If the prospect says that there is nothing else, your case is further strengthened.

Smoke Out

"[Prospect's Name], if I can satisfy you completely on that point, would you have any objection to going ahead with this purchase today?" If your prospect says that there is another stumbling block, you should reply, "Well, then, there must be something else in the back of your mind. Would you mind sharing it with me?" In your dialogue, be sure to "smoke out" any more hidden objections.

Boomerang

"Sorry, [Prospect's Name], I'm too busy; I can't see you." The boomerang will put the ball back in the prospect's court.

SALES PROFESSIONAL: "[Prospect's Name], you're busy, I'm busy. Why do think I'm calling you? To arrange a mutually convenient time when the two of us can get together, when you're not going to be so busy. You'll then be able to have a relaxing time with me."

What you are doing is fading the objection back to the prospect, but in a positive manner.

PROSPECT: "I can't afford it."
SALES PROFESSIONAL: "You can't afford it? [Prospect's Name], you cannot afford to be without it. That's why we should be sitting down."

Admit and Compensate

Sometimes, you will get a valid objection, and you ought to admit its validity. Don't even try to skirt around it. Don't come up with any fancy footwork. Compensate for the objection by admitting the *Three Fs: Feel, Felt, Found.*

"I understand how you feel. Quite frankly, others have felt the same way. But we have found. . . ."

"[Prospect's Name], I'm with you. I understand how you feel, because I feel it, too. Others felt the same way until I found a way that would allow them to. . . ."

Four Basic Objections

Most sales training courses will classify objections as being in one of four categories: (1) no need, (2) no hurry, (3) no money, or (4) no confidence. A sales professional who can anticipate the prospect's objection will be one step ahead of the buying game. If anticipation isn't possible, the sales professional needs to determine the exact nature of the prospect's objections, and then respond appropriately to overcome them.

1. *No need.* Typical "no-need" objections may sound like this: "You know, I have a product like this that I purchased a few years back. While your product does have nice features, I'm not sure I need it."

The sales professional has to determine whether the prospect's objection is a pure lack of motivation to buy, a lack of understanding, or a fear of facing a need. If there is a lack of motivation to buy, the sales professional may not have a prospect and should be prepared to move on. If a lack of understanding is perceived, the sales professional needs to go back and reestablish the commitments the prospect made before the sales professional started to close the sale. If the problem is denial, the sales professional must establish the reality of the need and the economic impact it could have on the prospect, personally or professionally.

2. *No hurry.* The "no-hurry" objections are almost always attempts to put off the inevitable. Be clear with these objections. Say, "I don't want to be the kind of sales professional who is so persistent that I become persona non grata, so if you'd like me to back off, tell me, and we'll forget this." You can't lose something you never had.

When you give them room, most prospects will come back and say; "Oh no! I still want to do this, but I can't right now." You can then coax the prospect to help you understand why. If you listen carefully, the prospect's explanation usually will tell you how to sell him or her.

The key, for the sales professional, is to get the prospect to indicate the next step. The sales professional needs a commitment from the prospect. Eventually, the prospect will either buy or tell the sales professional that the sale is off. With patience and persistence, the sales professional will make the sale; the key is not to give up. The sales professional shouldn't throw in the towel and let the prospect off the hook.

3. *No money.* This objection is much easier to handle than the first two. If the sales professional has done a good job of understanding the prospect's needs and situation, the buying recommendation will be within a range that the prospect can afford. The sales professional who believes that it is the right thing for the prospect to do will make the sale.

4. *No confidence.* The prospect who uses this objection usually needs more information. The sales professional's first step is to articulate clearly what he or she thinks the prospect is saying. By repeating what is heard, the sales professional assures the prospect he or she is carefully listening. Another benefit is that the prospect hears his or her own words repeated, which enables the prospect to evaluate whether what was said is what was really meant.

It is important for the sales professional to remember that these objections are the prospect's way of saying, "You haven't convinced me yet."

By dealing patiently with each objection, the sales professional establishes concern for the prospect. If the sales professional brushes off an objection, the prospect will conclude that the sales professional is more interested in making the sale than in helping the prospect to do the best thing.

Objections as Expressions of Fear

An objection is nothing more than an expression of the prospects' fear: fear of being oversold, fear of being unable to make payments over time, fear of making a mistake, or fear of buying from the wrong company or person. If sales professionals can discover the things that the prospects fear, they can help prospects express their fears and, ultimately, overcome them. If sales professionals ignore their prospects' fears, the prospects will not trust them and will find another way, or another salesperson, to resolve their fears.

Remember that objections are part of the sales process. Sales professionals should not make them out to be bigger than they really are. Sales professionals simply have to listen and evaluate what their prospects are really saying. A sales professional's role is to be a facilitator—to help prospects assess their needs and determine whether the products and services they offer will help meet those needs better than other alternatives. First and foremost, sales professionals must help prospects understand their own needs.

Most often, prospects are merely asking for help in understanding and overcoming the fear of making a mistake. Sales professionals who look at an objection as anything other than a natural part of the sales process are giving the objection more power than it requires or deserves.

Objections as Symptoms

Most objections can be prevented if the sales process is followed properly. There are only a few typical reasons for objections:

1. Not enough benefits are apparent to the prospect. The benefits may be there, but either the prospect has not heard them or they have not been presented clearly.

2. The objection response is simply a habit, a conditioned response that serves as a defense mechanism or a stall tactic when the prospect senses a sales situation.

3. The prospect uses the objection as a way to get rid of the sales professional because he or she has no time for a sales call or dislikes the sales professional or the company he or she represents.

4. The prospect fears making a wrong decision—thus the claim that more "shopping" needs to be done.

5. The prospect simply does not understand the presentation of the products or services.

6. People are naturally resistant to change.

Fortunately, all of these reasons can be anticipated and solved at various stages in a properly followed sales process. It is extremely important that you have an answer for any objection that comes your way. Memorize as many of the responses as you can. Even more important, be mindful that a raw response, used improperly or out of context, can destroy a sale as much as giving no response at all. Using responses improperly refers to the manner in which they are employed, which includes attitude, tone of voice, and body language. Using responses out of context refers to failure to integrate them with a properly sequenced sales process.

Although each sales scenario is, in a sense, unique, most will follow a fairly standard process. Well-accepted components of the process—the initial building of positive rapport, conducting a thorough fact finder, determining goals and objectives, uncovering needs and/or problems, presenting solutions, and closing—are there for you as guideposts toward maintaining confident control of your prospect and resolving any concerns he or she may have about your recommendations.

Objections as Clues to Closing

Do you view an objection as an insurmountable end or as a tool to help you close the sale? For many sales professionals, objections are merely methods of communication. A "No" doesn't mean "No, never." It merely means that prospects didn't say "Yes." Why? Perhaps you failed to properly communicate solutions to your prospects' problems. Perhaps they don't understand and accept the existence of their problems.

Preparation is vital to the sales process. It is important to understand and anticipate all the possible objections that you might receive—and to have in place the direction that you will follow in handling these concerns.

Objections are opportunities. Recall the phrase, "One man's garbage is another man's treasure." To some sales professionals, the objection appears to be a huge stumbling block. To others, it is a request for more information. The objection offers an opportunity to present some additional features of your products or services or to clarify and expand the perception of some features already mentioned but not clearly understood.

Objections give you feedback. You should welcome your prospects' comments because their feedback shows that they are thinking about what you are selling. In fact, you should always commend them for their excellent questions or statements. By receiving feedback, you will know the direction in which their thinking is headed. It's better to have prospects voice their concerns, rather than hide them and just say "No" to the proposal without explaining why.

Objections give clues to closing the sale; they reveal what points are most important to prospects. When you successfully handle their questions, you can ask them to take positive action.

Do your prospects view your handling of their concerns and questions as persuasion or propaganda? You can successfully persuade someone to accept a different point of view through the use of examples, additional information, documentation, and logic.

The use of stories and examples allows prospects to see the answers to or the consequences of their objections as applied to someone else, without getting hurt themselves. They will feel that they can learn from the experiences of others, without being in a defensive mood. Stories relax the tension of the moment and shift prospects' attention to the people in the story. When you don't have stories of your own to share, don't be afraid to borrow them from other sales professionals. Over the years, you will build up many stories. You don't have to tell prospects the moral of a story; they will draw the conclusions themselves. You are not persuading them; they are persuading themselves.

One MDRT sales associate can attest to this strategy:

Recently, I was working with three owners of a car dealership in Arizona. I strongly urged them to enact a buy/sell agreement funded with life insurance. They all agreed to sign the agreement and to purchase the insurance. The applications were signed and the initial premium paid. However, due to procrastination, one of the three postponed his physical. Before the physical could be taken, he and his wife were killed in a small plane crash. Not only was the insurance not in force, but they had not gotten around to signing the agreement. By will, his young children owned a third of the business. A car dealership has a need for a continuing line of credit. The young children and their guardian refused to sign any more notes. The resulting chaos forced the business into bankruptcy within 30 days.

Would you like to be in business with your partner's young children? This true story has helped the MDRT sales professional motivate others to take action immediately.

Another technique of persuasion is to introduce additional data or information, which will give prospects more input to evaluate: "Based on the original data presented, I see why you feel the way you do. However, with this additional information, you may feel differently." It lends credibility to your recommendations if you are able to produce more facts and statistics as backup.

Here's another MDRT sales professional's example, to bring this point home:

Let's say my prospect objects to buying life insurance and says, "My wife can remarry." My answer would be, "That's what I used to think until I actually saw recent remarriage statistics. According to actuarial figures, the experience of the industry on remarriage of widows after age 30 on a ten-year basis is as follows: Age 30—403 of every 1,000 remarry; age 40—193 of every 1,000 remarry; age 50—86 out of every 1,000 remarry; age 60—46 of every 1,000 remarry."

What these figures do not disclose to prospects is the percentage of the remarrying women who have children. Widows who have young children will have difficulty in finding a man who is willing to take on the support of these children. Note that less than 20 percent of widows in the 40- to 50-year-old age bracket remarry. Not too promising a picture.

Your presentations can be one-page proposals, or you can take your computer with you to support the analysis, calculations, and documentation involved with any of the products you sell. This won't be needed in most interviews, but the backup is there if needed.

Sometimes, a discussion of logic will persuade prospects. When prospects raise objections, maybe they haven't thought out the ramifications of a particular course of action. By raising questions and logically analyzing the possible pitfalls and consequences, they will often answer their own objections.

Your response to objections will be viewed as propaganda if you get into an argument with a prospect. In arguing, you don't introduce new information; you become more assertive about the same facts. This causes prospects to become more defensive and to close their minds. You may win the battle, but you will lose the war. If you get the feeling that an argument could result or that prospects are closing up, you can shift directions and ease tensions by introducing a story.

Propaganda involves not listening to what prospects are saying or mistakenly responding with "canned" answers not tailored to the prospects' situations. Some sales professionals try to intimidate prospects. If prospects buy through intimidation, they will likely have a short-lived relationship as customers.

The proper handling of objections is really one step in the total process of meeting your prospects' needs. Each step evolves into another, leading to the successful purchase of the products you sell. This natural evolution is planned by sales professionals. The first step is to establish the relationship—to achieve a free flow of dialogue, and have your prospects feel comfortable about sharing any thoughts they may have. You want prospects to know that you are empathetic and caring. Throughout your sales interview, you want to maintain this relationship and never let it degenerate into a conflict.

The sales interview may appear to be somewhat unstructured, even though you know exactly where you are headed. This lack of structure will tend to relax your prospects, make them feel more comfortable, and make the interview more personalized.

Try to fully develop your prospects' needs in their present situation. By dramatizing their needs, they know the consequences of inaction. In a way, you want to disturb them so that they have to do something to get their lives back into equilibrium. Most of the interview may be spent in the problem-fixing stage. You can then be your prospects' "assistant buyer"—helping them figure out the best course of action to solve their problems. If they hesitate or object, go back to the problems that will not go away. Then they are arguing with the problems, not with you. You will be there to help them consider all the alternatives of each course of action.

Try to anticipate all possible objections. You may even introduce some, and answer them, during the presentation or problem-setting stage. You may prepare to handle others with additional information or examples when and if they come up. By bringing up the objections yourself, you have the advantage of phrasing them in the way that is easiest for the prospect to handle. You may show prospects that you have identified and considered all the alternatives.

Your sales creed should teach you that you will always do for prospects what you would do for yourself if you were in their position. If this philosophy is applied to all of your business dealings, your recommendations will carry the weight of conviction.

You must believe that what you are recommending is correct and proper. Once you are convinced of that, you earnestly strive to make prospects understand why it is the best course of action. "[Prospect's Name], it is more important for you to own this product than it is for me to sell it. I don't care whom you buy this type of product from, but please, for *your* benefit, buy it!"

Chapter 5

Phrases That Will Help You Close

MDRT sales professionals employ what has come to be called the "the power phrase"—a sentence or phrase that crystallizes an important idea and nudges the prospect closer to a positive decision to buy. The Power Phrases listed later in this chapter are perfectly adaptable to any sales situation in any industry.

Power Talking: What You Say Is What You Get

1. *Powerless-language opening.* The sales professional who walks into a room to conduct a seminar appears nervous, moves tentatively, and speaks with a wishy-washy inflection.

> Gosh, well, I'm a little nervous about being here in front of all of you people, and I sure hope you won't be disappointed in what I have to say. For the most part, it's just common sense that you've probably already heard before, so I just hope it won't be too boring. Let's just go ahead and get started.

2. *Hyped-up, phony-language opening.* The sales professional pirouettes, then faces the audience again with an eager expression and motion-filled body language.

Wow, is it ever a pleasure to be with you! It sure is a good thing you chose this session this afternoon, because the next 30 minutes will totally change your career and your life. To be perfectly honest, you have never heard *about* any products and services as important as the ones I'm about to explain here today. I can't wait to get started, so let's begin!

3. *Sincere-language opening.* The sales professional faces the audience, pauses until paper rustling and conversations stop, and then uses genuine body language and a normal speaking tone.

I feel privileged to be here with you; each one of you is a strong representative of your community. Your being here today shows a genuine interest in the products and services I sell. My aims in this seminar are to help you understand the product benefits and to show you how these products can be used for maximum results. Let's get started.

As you read these three openings, you probably had a distinctly different reaction to each one of them. Did you feel, very early in the first opening, that you would have made a big mistake in choosing this seminar?

When you read the second opening, did you have the impression that you were about to get a "snow job"?

From just a few sentences, you made some very rapid and valid conclusions about what your presenter would be like. Your prospective clients are doing exactly the same thing when they talk with you. They size you up based on how you present yourself. This chapter will show you the best ways to present yourself most positively.

Three fundamental principles form the crux of power talking:

1. The people you meet, work with, and sell to, quickly size you up every time you speak, whether you're phoning to schedule an appointment with a prospect, sitting down next to another passenger on a flight home, or meeting a new neighbor. You can dramatically change and improve the image you are currently projecting, simply by changing a few of your phrases and words.

2. The prospects who (you hope) will cooperate with you, help you, and buy from you, take cues from your language; then they decide whether they'll go along with you or work against you. You can gain and enhance their willingness to cooperate by the way you talk with them.

3. Listen to yourself. The language and phrases you use when talking with others help to mold your own self-image, and ultimately determine how and whether you will attain success in the pursuit of your goals. You win or lose with the words you choose. Your words, thoughts, and actions are all interrelated; they all play a role in attaining the achievements you seek. Your words are the easiest to alter and have the most immediate effect. When you consciously set out to change your words, everything else changes, too.

Let's start by shaping the image you project to others. Changing a few common phrases can dramatically change the way you come across to others.

Replace "I'll have to" with "I'll be glad to." General Electric's state-of-the-art "Telephone Answer Center" in Louisville, Kentucky, was recently featured on *60 Minutes*. It's dedicated to projecting a positive, friendly, helpful image for the company. Each day, on average, each telephone rep answers 96 phone calls, and each call averages three requests for information—for example, "What colors are available for a [model/type] dishwasher?"

or, "How much electricity does a [model/type] pump use?" or "How come my microwave makes fireworks every time I try to preheat my pewter plates?"

When GE asked an outside consultant to train its staff, the consultant stressed the need to replace the phrase "I'll have to" with something more along the lines of "I'll be glad to" when responding to callers. Customers noticed the difference, and they consistently rave about their positive experiences in calling GE. How do your clients and prospects feel when you say: "I'll have to pull your file to check your account status, then I'll have to contact my corporate sales office. I'll have to call you back this afternoon with the answer." Would they notice a difference if you said: "I'd like to pull your file to check your account status, then I'll be happy to contact the corporate sales office to get clarification. I'll be glad to call you back this afternoon with the answer."

They'll notice the difference, and you will, too. If you were a GE telephone rep and heard yourself, all day long—288 times a day, in fact, if you were handling 96 calls with three requests each—saying "I'll have to," "I'll have to," "I'll have to," you'd feel discouraged and resentful by the end of the day.

The same advice applies to your daily conversations with clients and prospects, colleagues, and sales office personnel. Replace "I'll have to" with "I'll be glad to," to project a more positive and friendly image, and to help yourself feel more positive throughout the day.

Eliminate "integrity busters." What's your first thought when you hear, "Well, I'll be honest with you . . . "? Do you wonder whether the person has been less than honest until now? If you meet with a prospect and say, "I've looked over the product you now have, and, well, to tell you the truth . . . ," it sounds like you're not always truthful. To project a high-integrity image, eliminate all those habitual phrases like, "I'll level with you" or "To be perfectly candid." They make you sound as if you're issuing a special notice that you're about to be honest, because it's such unusual behavior for you! Your long-term reputation is what counts in the sales profession. Always be honest, and drop any habitual phrases that suggest you aren't.

Dispense with "self-belittlers." A tiny word like "just" or "only" can project an image that's exactly the opposite of what you want to convey. Two finalist candidates were interviewing for an important marketing position with a major telecommunications company. Both had received the same set of interview questions two days before meeting with the selection panel.

One began, "I've only had two days to look over your questions, so these are just my initial reactions to what you're looking for, and I may be way off. Unfortunately, I really just don't have any firsthand experience in your industry, so I'll just do my best."

The other candidate said, "I've had two full days to look over your questions, and I'll be glad to give you my best thinking on how to handle the situations you've asked about. Fortunately, I bring firsthand experience from a totally different industry, so I'll take a fresh, unconventional approach to your business."

The second candidate got the nod and the job. Her actual answers weren't any better, but she had put them, and herself, in a much more favorable light by eliminating self-belittling phrases like "I'm just" or "I'm only."

You will project a more consistently positive and confident image by eliminating any words that denigrate your experience or qualifications. A meeting with a prospective client is a lot like a job interview. The prospect is sizing you up, deciding whether to hire you as the new insurance and financial consultant.

Encourage more cooperation and sales by eliminating conflict. All sales professionals could use a little more cooperation from others, especially in selling situations. Clients who depend on them to make reliable recommendations want to feel that sales professionals are competent advisers who are working in their best interests. Unfortunately, language patterns can get in the way of developing and perpetuating the atmosphere of cooperation sales professionals need. Get that "but" out of your statements. "Frank is an MDRT member and is a superb agent, but he wears a beard." "Frank is an MDRT member and is a superb agent, and he wears a beard." What's the difference between those two statements? That one word, "but," makes all the difference. It's an eraser word. Whatever you've just heard is erased as soon as you hear "but." If someone says to you, "You're doing a fine job developing your territory, but . . ." it immediately makes you feel defensive because you can tell that there's a big qualifier coming. You're much better off to substitute "and" for "but" so the person you're talking with keeps an open mind— and keeps listening to and working with you.

Replace "disagree" with "understand." Another conflict word that's closely related to "but," and sometimes used with it, is "disagree." This tricky word changes meaning as it passes from your lips to your listener's ear. You say the word "disagree," and they think they hear you saying, "You're wrong!" You may say, "I can understand that you feel a half-million-dollar policy will give you sufficient protection, but I disagree . . ." What they hear is, "You're wrong! Your belief is ill-informed. You're dumb."

Rather than saying "I disagree," substitute this statement: "I understand, and here's another point of view we should consider." This keeps the options open and eliminates a conflict situation in which one of you must prevail. After all, you're working together as partners to come up with the best protection plan. By creating a cooperative atmosphere, you may, together, come up with a third approach that's different from and better than either of the positions you were considering before.

Invite others to choose among alternatives. Your very first sales seminar or tape program probably taught you the alternate-choice close, and it's always been a good tool in finalizing a sale. That's not all the alternate choice approach is good for, though. Whenever you want people to cooperate with you, they're much more likely to work with you if they have a choice among alternatives.

Always offer your clients and prospects choices to select from. They'll be more cooperative and more committed to their choices because they have some personal ownership in the course they've chosen.

Enhance your own self-image by purging phrases that negatively affect your thinking and arrest your success. Prospects and clients aren't the only ones who hear and pay attention to your phrasing. You hear yourself, too, and your choices of words and phrases influence how you feel about yourself. Psychotherapists, in fact, use a technique called "cognitive restructuring" to change patients' views of themselves by altering their language patterns. You don't have to be in therapy to benefit from continuously enhancing your own self-image by changing your language.

Convert "failures" into "lessons." Let's face it, sales professionals didn't get to MDRT by succeeding all the time. They went through a lot of approaches that didn't work very well, and met with scores of prospects who turned out not to be prospects after all, despite their qualification process. And, they've also lost plenty of business that they should have retained. Along with their successes, they've had many failures. In fact, without them, they wouldn't have become the accomplished winners that they are.

Henry Ford's definition of "failure" has hit home for many sales professionals:

> "Failure is the opportunity to begin again, more intelligently." You will continue to have lots of failures along the road to success. To ensure that they are beneficial experiences that help you improve and excel, it is recommended that you replace the phrase "I failed" with "I learned."

Rather than saying, "The meeting didn't go well at all. I failed to develop enough rapport right up front, so he didn't really have an open mind in considering my proposal," use a more constructive recap: "Next time, the meeting will go a lot better. I learned, once again, that it's always critical to develop solid rapport right up front, so my prospect will keep an open mind in considering my proposals."

Every failure presents a lesson. Focus on what you can learn from a failure, and you come out ahead. Concentrate on it and you get stuck in negativity, while denying yourself the positive education that will help ensure that the same setback doesn't happen again.

Replace "If only I had" with "Starting now, I will." Losers focus on what has gone wrong in the past—what hasn't worked. Winners keep their sights focused on the future. A man in his mid-40s described a bedside conversation he had with his kids when he was recovering from a heart attack. When he said, "If only I hadn't let myself get so stressed out," his kids reminded him that his recovery couldn't really begin until he shifted his attention toward what he was going to do differently in the future. Their comments prompted him to change his edict to himself: "As soon as I'm released, I'm going to be much more attentive to my diet, and I'll begin a sensible exercise program. Starting now, I'll begin to manage my stress and begin keeping my priorities in a more realistic perspective." That's when his recovery really began.

All of us make mistakes, both professionally and personally. They're inevitable. But how we respond to them determines what our future will be like. You can consistently guide yourself to greater levels of personal and professional success by eliminating regrets and thinking about what you'll do differently in the future. Get rid of your own look-back-over-the-shoulder phrases, like "If only I had," and replace them with change-oriented language, like "Starting now, I will."

Say "I will," not "I'll try." You've been hearing about the difference between "I'll try" and "I will" throughout much of your career, but have you completely eliminated that wishy-washy "I'll try" from your vocabulary? When a prospect hears you say, "I'll try to get that price out to you today," or "I'll try to call you next week," he or she knows better than to rely on your follow-through. Instead, use language that shows your commitment. Remember, it's not just the other person who hears you; you hear yourself, too. When you hear yourself say, "I will call you next week," you encourage yourself to live up to your own commitments and keep building your track record of reliability.

Incidentally, one key to delighting (rather than just satisfying) clients is to consistently exceed their expectations. When you make commitments, you're always wise to build in a little safety cushion. Make commitments that you're positive you can keep and you're also pretty sure you can beat. If you think you can complete a review by Wednesday, don't say, "I can probably complete this by Wednesday." You're much better off to say, "I will complete the product review before the end of the week"— and then still do your best to complete it by Wednesday. In that way, you'll probably exceed your prospect's expectations, and you're certain to at least meet them, rather than take a chance on letting him or her down if unexpected conflicts prevent you from finishing on Wednesday.

And speaking of "trying," should you "try" to put these power-talking phrases to work in your daily conversations? Absolutely not. *Do* it, don't try. And right now is the perfect time to start.

Certain phraseology may prove beneficial in your appointments. One that seems to work very well is: "[Prospect's Name], not everyone needs this product." The typical response is: "Why would someone *not* need it?" Ah ha! Now it gets interesting. The more reasons you find that someone does not need your product, the more you reinforce that your prospect does need it.

Another phrase that seems to get good response, and usually a silent response, is: "I'm in this business for the long haul. I hope to be working with you 20 years from now." Corny? Maybe. Honest? Yes. And the silent response is the best kind.

Here's another: "Let me show you the best product first and if that does not work, we can look at other products." Your prospect will probably think, "An inferior product? Never! I want the best product."

The rest of this chapter consists of power phrases that you can adapt and use in your closing deliveries.

Power Phrases

In any discussions with prospects, power phrases are highly effective for getting your point across. Power phrases convey ideas in concise language and with precise meaning. They are readily understood and easy to retain.

It's wise to modify power phrases so that you feel comfortable using them and they fit your style. Words, properly used, are great sales associates in and of themselves. And when the right words are strung together to form strong phrases, they become super sales vehicles. To substantiate this point, let's take a few effective power phrases as examples. The first phrase is "inevitable gain." How nice it is to be able to say to prospects, when they buy your product, "There is an inevitable gain when you purchase this." "Saving money" is another. These two simple words form a very powerful phrase: "When you buy my product, you're not spending money—you're saving money." "How much would you like to save this month?" "You can save dollars, quarters, nickels, dimes, $10 bills, $100 bills—it's all up to you."

The long list of power phrases that follows has been used over the years by some of the MDRT's most successful sales associates. Each phrase is simple, but when used in the right situation, it can be the best tool to help you close your sales.

✓ My business separates true sales professionals from good imitators. Those with persistence will succeed. Those who are easily discouraged will not.

✓ Be an agent of action, not an actor affected by events.

✓ You won't know whether you won if you don't keep score.

✓ Opportunities only come about because of the many years of groundwork I've laid.

✓ Selling is a combination of logic and motivation.

✓ Develop a reputation of integrity and dependability.

✓ Success is believing that what you're doing is worthwhile and that doing it well is what really matters.

✓ There will always be room for the sales professional who calls on a person in need.

✓ Be prepared to work 12- to 14-hour days during your first five years.

✓ I live on the trust I establish in the community.

✓ Do the important rather than the urgent. I sell a product that is very important to people but never seems very urgent.

✓ After all is said and done, financial success is measured in profits—not in volume.

✓ You are the crucial link between your company and your clients.

✓ If you had a brain tumor, would you want a part-time surgeon doing your operation?

✓ Do you value your reputation as a good businessperson?

✓ One can be in business for 10 years and have 10 years of experience or one year's experience 10 times.

✓ We need to keep an open mind, especially with things changing so fast in our industry.

✓ Pride and achievement, not money, keep me working.

✓ How you handle yourself on your bad days will determine your success in this business.

✓ We must remember that we are paid to be problem solvers.

✓ There are two things that do not last—dogs that chase cars, and sales professionals without appointments.

✓ The level of your success is dependent on your level of caring, sharing, and giving.

✓ Everyone has the right to be heard—but you have to earn the right to be taken seriously.

✓ Become a specialist. Identify a population of clients with whom you feel comfortable.

✓ Be daring, first, and different.

✓ If you don't act professionally, you won't have your business.

✓ You have to establish your expertise and develop a level of trust before you can begin selling a client anything.

✓ I am a good person to know because I care about my clients, their families, and their businesses.

✓ There is always more than one way to town. The successful sales professional will find it.

✓ Your percentage of successful closes, multiplied by your number of attempted sales, multiplied by your average case size, will determine your production.

✓ We are in the business of taking away—tearing off the veneer and breaking through the communication barriers to expose the prospect.

✓ A sales professional has to deserve the sale he or she gets.

✓ If the fun ever goes out of my work, I'll quit doing it.

✓ A good job, with the client always first in your thoughts, pays better than anything else you can do.

✓ Success for me means success for my clients.

✓ I am assertive. But I'm successful because my clients are my friends.

✓ Would my competitor's representative be visiting with you on this cold and rainy winter's night?

✓ I'm in this business for the long haul. I hope to be working with you 20 years from now.

✓ We must realize that our job is not one of education but of moving people to action.

✓ The best sales professionals I know push the hardest. They know the sale is their responsibility.

✓ A successful sales professional is born with a capacity to become "other-person-centered."

✓ Many people do not know what they do not know. My job is to help them know.

✓ If you asked 1,000 successful sales professionals how they do it, you'll get 1,000 different answers.

✓ Every year I get more involved, and every year my production goes up.

✓ We are the professional futurists—without our products and services, there will be no future for many.

✓ Change seems to be inevitable. How we cope with it is the measure of our survival and our success.

✓ If it were suddenly a crime to sell your product, could the D.A. gather enough evidence to convict you?

✓ Nice guys finish first . . . and they last!

✓ I am always there as a sounding board for my clients.

✓ Success is a good bottom line.

✓ I am the same average sales professional at 200 cases as I was at 80.

✓ Sales professionals don't fail in the business, they just stop trying.

✓ Consecutive weekly production builds the inventory of our stock-in-trade.

✓ Don't tell your clients how good you are; let them catch you at it.

✓ We have all experienced the agony of rejection and the ecstasy of acceptance.

✓ Integrity—it's your number-one asset. Don't risk it!

✓ The recipe for a good speech usually includes shortening.

✓ The deposit window is too close to the withdrawal window.

✓ The next time you make a bank deposit, will you become bank-account-poor?

✓ I am here to discuss those things that your corporation can do more effectively for you than you can do for yourself.

✓ The three words a business owner knows best: "profit," "wholesale," and "retail."

✓ When judging the merits of a company, it's more important to look at its historic performance than to look at its predictions on an illustration.

✓ Never spend a commission before it's paid.

✓ When the sales professional needs the commission more than the prospect needs the product, both the sales professional and the prospect are in trouble.

✓ The first sale to a person is rarely the big one; we tend to get paid later.

✓ The sweetness of low price is soon forgotten, but the bitterness of low quality lingers on.

✓ The best way to keep your clients is not to give them away.

✓ When you *know* you know, you fear no person.

✓ Remember, if it sounds too good to be true, it probably is!

✓ It is time we gave the critics and our competition a deaf ear and continue to go about our business.

✓ It amazes me that many of my contemporaries folded their tents at age 65.

✓ If the grass is greener on the other side of the fence, chances are the water bill is higher too.

✓ Selling quality products is an effective means of insulating my clients from my competition.

✓ The sweetness of low price never equals the sourness of poor quality.

✓ Our work is not easy, and for that we should be grateful. If it were, there would be far more people trying to chase the same amount of business, and that really could be tough.

✓ In the end, it pays to have the best in the beginning.

✓ Goodwill is the one and only asset that competition cannot undersell or destroy.

✓ Find out what everybody else is doing—then don't do it.

✓ You never know you are in competition until you lose the case.

✓ You never know how good you are until you get up against the best.

✓ Do you want the product you buy to be there when you need it the most?

✓ You solve permanent problems with permanent solutions.

✓ If consumers understood my product as I do, they would buy it over the counter.

✓ Learning to use a personal computer takes time, practice, and patience, but the time is well worth it.

✓ The future will always belong to the informed.

✓ A person's judgment is no better than his or her information.

✓ Continuing education is a basic ingredient for continuing success.

✓ There is never a point in a selling career at which the sales professional can stop learning or studying.

✓ Knowledge is power. Knowledge coupled with marketing ability spells success.

✓ The size of the market is determined by the space between the sales professional's ears.

✓ Continuing education in the selling business is what sharpening an axe is to wood cutting.

✓ A vital ingredient to success is a willingness to learn.

✓ Continuing education and persistence overcome all obstacles.

✓ No individual has a monopoly on knowledge.

✓ If you are not expandable, you are expendable.

✓ It's not just one economic crisis after another anymore. Every once in a while there's a disaster.

✓ If you think education is expensive, try ignorance and pay forever.

✓ I don't regard clients as clients until they have bought from me twice and thought of me first for advice.

✓ As never before, the sales professional has an impressive inventory to satisfy the needs of most clients.

✓ You had this problem before we met. My job is to help you solve it.

✓ I'm supposed to help you solve problems, not cause problems.

✓ We recognize and welcome the changing selling environment. Inherent in change are the seeds for growth.

✓ The greatest good you can do for others is not just to share with them your riches, but to reveal to them their own.

✓ If income isn't allocated, it will be spent.

✓ No company has a lease on the best product in all categories. You're obligated to seek out the best product.

✓ I owe my company the information from the marketplace that it needs to make its marketing decisions.

✓ You have to know what your market is.

✓ The framework created by laws and regulations is also an opportunity to be creative.

✓ When entering the sales business, the most important thing is service, service, service.

✓ Inflation is the reason you should have purchased this last year.

✓ What happens in the event of inflation?

✓ Have you heard about inflation? Well, my product is practically inflation-proof.

✓ Mr./Ms. Prospect, there are sad, dumb, and smart ways to use my product—let's talk.

✓ The key to a sale is an interview. The key to an interview is a disturbing question.

✓ Ad-libbing is for amateurs.

✓ Is there any particular part of what we talked about that makes you hesitate?

✓ Mr./Ms. Client, I need your help.

✓ The nearest to perfection most people ever come is during an introduction.

✓ By asking the right questions, you'll make the sale without any statements or proposing anything.

✓ I let my prospects tell me what they want and need. They will do so if I ask the right questions and listen to the answers.

✓ Nothing happens until you put yourself in front of a prospect in an interview.

✓ All you have in an interview is trust. Once violated, you have nothing.

✓ I stay away from business during our first meeting and just talk about things in general. I talk about the number of people I've helped and about serving, not being served.

✓ Slam-dunk your sales interview with a basic needs presentation.

✓ Before we proceed, I don't want to dig the hole for somebody else to put the pool in!

✓ You never get a second chance to make a first impression.

✓ At the end of every sales interview, I say, "Oh, by the way."

✓ Interviews to a sales professional are what fertilizer is to the crops. They produce a better yield.

✓ If you are not here when I return, whom should I ask for?

✓ The product is only as good as we are—neither it nor the price should become the focus of the interview.

✓ Is there any reason why we shouldn't consummate this purchase now?

✓ Closing a case begins at the beginning; it begins with your first contact.

✓ As far as I'm concerned, the sale is closed before I get there.

✓ You have knowledge and ideas that the consumer needs and wants. You are the added value.

✓ Find the facts first.

✓ The person who has all the answers is usually the one doing the least amount of talking.

✓ Are you going to talk to your spouse with a decision or for a decision?

✓ As long as you can write a check on your money, it doesn't make any difference what bank it's in, does it?

✓ Your banker believes in it, why don't you?

✓ Mr./Ms. Accountant, our clients wanted to buy this product. If you'd like to see it bought in a different way, we'll be glad to consider your way.

✓ Overcoming objections starts when you overcome your fears and your prejudices.

✓ There are only four objections: I don't believe in this product. I can't afford this product. I don't need this product. This product is a lousy investment. The others are variations on these four.

✓ Don't answer objections—play to win!

✓ Get the client to verbalize his or her objections.

✓ An objection is an opportunity to close.

✓ Always answer objections with "Yes, but . . . ."

✓ View any joint case as a temporary partnership. As in any partnership, the rules should be determined in advance.

✓ If two agents want to work together, it's important that they bring assets to the relationship.

✓ Most people don't like to buy, but they love to own.

✓ No one has the power you have to affect the lives of your family—now.

✓ You don't have to buy an afternoon paper to find out what our product is worth.

✓ You just haven't needed it yet. Do you carry a spare tire in your automobile?

✓ Has our product kept pace with your family and business obligations?

✓ Put a floor beneath a little bit of tomorrow.

✓ What do you want our product or service to do for you?

✓ It takes character for one to buy my product for his or her family, and one thing we do not sell is character.

✓ You can't afford not to have it.

✓ People buy my product for two reasons: love and obligation. They either want to or have to. Forget the rest.

✓ Never look for bargains in parachutes, brain surgeons, or my product.

✓ My product is like the air conditioner in your car. It may not be tax-deductible, but it does make the ride a lot more comfortable.

✓ It is character that buys my product.

✓ Better to have it and not need it, than to need it and not have it.

✓ We should be proud of our product—there is no substitute for it.

✓ Do you have any prejudices for or against any particular type of product?

✓ My product doesn't cost, it pays.

✓ Does your product measure up to what you want it to do for you?

✓ Your need for my product never changes—it's the reasons you need it that change.

✓ My product isn't an added obligation—it's the best means of meeting the obligations you already have.

✓ Buying my product is like buying a truck. You don't like or dislike it. You use it.

✓ My product will probably not be the greatest investment you ever make, but it will be far from the worst.

✓ People who spare now, won't despair later.

✓ Our primary purpose is to help people—and if we can't help them, never to hurt them.

✓ Our business is like a game of tennis. We are given the racket and balls, but we must set up our own match.

✓ Selling our product is really helping people to help themselves.

✓ You can get everything in life you want, if you help enough people get what they want.

✓ If this business were easy, everyone would be doing it.

✓ It is our privilege to sell a product where the purchaser always benefits.

✓ Selling is not an intellectual exercise—it's an emotional exercise.

✓ The sales business is the epitome of the free enterprise system, and I'm proud to be part of it.

✓ We must be in the right business, because everyone else in the world is trying to get into it.

✓ We change if to when.

✓ I sell only what people need to buy.

✓ The more successful a person becomes, the greater his or her debt to our industry—and no person should remain haughty over that which makes him or her a debtor.

✓ Our job is to hold the hands of the successful and powerful.

✓ Don't be afraid to say that you're a sales professional. I'm proud of it.

✓ Give yourself to your career and it will give back the fruits of success and the knowledge that you can make things happen.

✓ All you sell is trust. Once that is violated, you have nothing.

✓ Do you consider your present occupation your lifetime work?

✓ I look at my product as a ministry of sorts.

✓ The business really does get better and better each year. The opportunities are unlimited for those sales professionals who are willing to pay the price to be the best.

✓ This business was always one of the most rejection-oriented businesses ever.

✓ We sell ideas of predictability and permanence in an environment where real long-range planning seems to have gone by the wayside.

✓ I do not sell my product. I help people buy what they understand they need.

✓ We have nothing to sell but one idea—money for future delivery.

✓ This business never lets you get too big. It constantly humbles and challenges you.

✓ My role is that of a mirror, which I try to hold up to clients to allow them to see what they truly desire.

✓ I sincerely believe in the product I sell, and I love the thrill of the chase.

✓ If you can't fall in love with the sales business, then get out of it.

✓ If you want to make it in this business, all you have to do is last.

✓ The profession we have chosen demands the skill to serve and the will to sacrifice.

✓ Think for just a minute: If we go out of business, who's going to take our place?

✓ If you don't like my product, you don't like money.

✓ My product is property—valuable property.

✓ Do you want me to be honest—or diplomatic?

✓ Experience has shown that the only serious thinking a person does about my product is done while the agent is sitting in front of him or her. Let's go through this again.

✓ Make it negotiable.

✓ Is this enough for you?

✓ I sell discounted dollars—dollars for pennies apiece. They cost three cents per dollar per year. May I show you?

✓ Put me on your payroll.

✓ No one wants to be "substandard." "Special class" is infinitely less offensive and equally correct.

✓ People buy your mind and your ideas.

✓ Use the 3 R's—restate the objection, reassure, and resume.

✓ How important are these objectives [that I have outlined] to you?

✓ If I give you a good idea, you have an obligation to do business with me.

✓ Making a "No" a "Yes"—any reason we can't do it today?

✓ My job is to get you the best value for your money, which is never the cheapest or the most expensive, but one that is comfortably in the middle.

✓ You can lead a thirsty mule to water, but you can't make him drink.

✓ If it sounds too good to be true, it is.

✓ Successful selling is talking to the emotions and not the intellect.

✓ I never ask a client, "Did you understand that?" Instead, I ask, "Did I make myself clear?"

✓ I've learned sensitivity, and it helps in business. I've found that many sales are built on trust, not on product illusions.

✓ Mr./Ms. Prospect, here's a pen. You cut out what you don't want for your family.

✓ Have I said anything so far that you don't understand or that you disagree with?

✓ This business will not change my life, but it could change yours or that of your family.

✓ Successful selling is the art of selling things that don't come back, to people who do.

✓ This might be your last opportunity to turn your objectives into reality.

✓ A person eats an apple one bite at a time. Take the kind of bite you can afford.

✓ Getting out and talking to people is the best cure for a sales slump.

✓ The first big factor in getting organized for sales is to spend time each day thinking about the things that have made other people star sales representatives, and following their systems.

✓ My responsibility to you as a client is to secure your future today.

✓ If you know a better way, use it. If you don't, you'd better use my method.

✓ Do not call on any prospects unless you are prepared to present at least one sound idea that they can use.

✓ After I make a suggestion or recommendation, I ask, "Do you object to that?"

✓ Since you have the good sense to make the right decisions at the right time, I am sure you will take this plan.

✓ All I'm going to do is help you and show you how you can protect against some of these contingencies.

✓ It really doesn't matter whether you're a physician or a ditchdigger. If you make half a million dollars, your needs are essentially the same.

✓ How much of this product were you planning on buying from your brother-in-law in the future? None. Then why are we talking about him?

✓ Give me the opportunity to earn the right to have you as a client.

✓ Which product do you like better? Product A or Product B?

✓ A sale is made out of every interview. Either they sell me on why they shouldn't buy or I sell them on why they should.

✓ People only buy what they understand.

✓ The biggest sale I have is to help my client focus on his or her objective.

✓ It's not what you *know* about selling, it's what you *do* about selling that counts.

✓ Sell what the product does, not what it is.

✓ Real estate = location, location, location. Sales = timing, timing, timing.

✓ You are never too smart to learn a new way to makes sales in the business.

✓ People buy my trust, not my products or services.

✓ Selling is telling the truth in an attractive and convincing manner.

✓ I will swap my service for your loyalty.

✓ If you don't understand it, don't buy it.

✓ Do you want to make it a must or a plus?

✓ Which part of this product don't you believe in?

✓ When you work out solutions with your client, the sale is being made in the process.

✓ Remember that when you show the cost of a product, you must also show a benefit.

✓ Don't sell needs, sell wants.

✓ Everyone says money talks. Listen to what my product is telling you!

✓ Sell the concept, not the numbers. The numbers will change—the concept won't.

✓ Mr./Ms. Prospect, why not solve your problems when things are going well?

✓ Help your prospects realize they are planting shade trees under which they may never sit.

✓ Why don't we take action now on this plan?

✓ When people invite you into their home or business, knowing full well what you do, they are saying, "I want to buy your product." But they won't make it easy. It's up to you to find out why.

✓ Please don't ask me to give you time, because all I can do is sell it to you.

✓ If you feel it is a good idea, then now is the time to make the decision. Tomorrow might be too late.

✓ Selling needs instead of price or products is my primary marketing thrust.

✓ I want it to be your fault that you didn't buy it—not mine that I didn't sell it.

✓ When I work for you, you get a lifetime guarantee.

✓ Find out what clients want—not what their accountants or lawyers want, but what clients want.

✓ Would you have any problem discussing your product needs with me?

✓ Always describe your product not as what it is, but what it does!

✓ A big case is just like a small case.

✓ Figure out what shape the hole is before you try to sell your peg.

✓ Get in the habit of trying to sell something in addition to the product or service you are proposing.

✓ Frankly, Mr./Ms. Prospect, I want you as a client.

✓ Successful people look for pleasing results—unsuccessful people look for pleasing methods.

✓ Have you ever done anything that is in the best interest of your family that you have regretted later?

✓ It is easier to convince someone to do something than to find someone who wanted to do it in the first place.

✓ There is a big difference between good sound reasons and reasons that sound good.

✓ Allow me to help you achieve what you are working for.

✓ With this plan, all of these benefits are our obligation. Without it, they become your obligation.

✓ You can't possibly pay me as much as I can pay you.

✓ Don't sell products, sell ideas.

✓ If you decide you want to pursue this, we'll make an appointment to spend some time.

✓ The personal touch will always be very important. No computer has ever sold a policy.

✓ Facts tell, emotion sells.

✓ Here is an idea you should be aware of.

✓ This plan is in your best interest. You should do it, today!

✓ It seems to me that you are doing it the hard way.

✓ I always felt that every *no sale* I made was another step away from failure.

✓ Sales success has two basic rules. 1. Stay on the phone. 2. Stay on the street.

✓ A sale takes place when there is a transfer of enthusiasm.

✓ Promise a lot and deliver more.

✓ The three most important letters in your sales presentation are: A-S-K.

✓ Concentrate on establishing the problem, not selling the solution.

✓ Do you have enough faith in your attorney or accountant to allow me to review their work?

✓ By purchasing this product, you are making better use of your dollars.

✓ Sales tracks feel awkward and rehearsed. But learn them anyway. What I use today is a little bit that I've borrowed out of language and ideas I didn't think were me. I put them all together and today it's my own sales approach.

✓ People respond much more readily to a stroke than to a stick.

✓ The only people who buy my products are people who have desire.

✓ Our approach is to narrow the range and sharpen the focus rather than broaden the range and blur the focus.

✓ Nothing is sold until it is understood.

✓ What I don't know I will find out for you.

✓ I don't have faith in anything I don't understand, either; let me show you how this works.

✓ Selling products and services is like playing tennis—you just hit it back one more time than your prospect.

✓ Your plans can be self-completing or self-destructing—it's your choice.

✓ I let clients talk—they may tell me something we both need to know!

✓ If you buy from me, you do not make me a millionaire. If you don't, you do not put me out of business.

✓ There is no substitute for motivated brains.

✓ Your power will be equal to your commitment.

✓ Time matures—success endures, through work, love, and a life of happiness.

✓ Winners win, losers make excuses.

✓ It's not what you can't do, it's what you can do.

✓ Fear vanishes when imagination ceases and action begins.

✓ I believe I belong to that group of people who, when challenged, work harder. Under pressure, we perform better.

✓ You need to realize that you can do far more than you thought you could.

✓ The most expensive thing a person can own is a closed mind.

✓ What you plant is what you reap; the sooner you plant, the sooner you harvest.

✓ It's not how many years in life but rather how much life in those years.

✓ Don't be afraid to think big!

✓ We need goals and deadlines—goals big enough to be exciting, and deadlines to make us run.

✓ Self-confidence is the best form of success.

✓ The things that a person thinks about the most are the things that he or she will do best.

✓ Most people don't plan to fail, they fail to plan.

✓ What the mind can conceive, the body can achieve.

✓ If you say you can, or if you say you can't, you're probably right.

✓ Doing the right thing is never wrong.

✓ Cheap things are rarely good, and good things are rarely cheap.

✓ Never be satisfied with what you have done today, for tomorrow can be a better day.

✓ A good deed never goes unrewarded.

✓ A good deed never goes unpunished.

✓ To try something where there is little hope of success is to risk failure, but to not try, guarantees it.

✓ Argue for your limitations and they are yours.

✓ Beware of the people who have the solution before they understand the problem.

✓ There is no known law by which you can achieve success without first expecting it.

✓ If you can get into the habit of writing down four things that you're thankful for every day, it will make you a better person.

✓ Life is worth living, people are worth loving, and God is worth trusting.

✓ Hope with expectancy.

✓ The key to success is to be a doer as well as a thinker.

✓ People can do amazing things—if they have amazing things to do!

✓ There is nothing so permanent as change.

✓ Every winner has a plan. Ever loser has an excuse.

✓ If you want to grow, add a zero.

✓ Fight for your highest obtainable gain, but never put up resistance in vain.

✓ Many receive advice, but only the wise profit from it.

✓ Tough problems never last, but tough people do.

✓ Winners make commitments, losers make promises.

✓ Move out, man! Life is fleeting. Do something worthwhile before you die; leave behind a work sublime that will outlive you and time.

✓ If nothing sings in you, you can't make music.

✓ You can have anything you want if you want it enough to get it.

✓ Tomorrow is the result of today, for the history of our todays inevitably determines our tomorrows.

✓ It's most important to do what we can, as best we can.

✓ Control is nothing more than control of oneself. It's knowing where we're going, and why we're going there.

✓ The best way to predict your future is to create it.

✓ Luck: Where knowledge and opportunity meet.

✓ Being broke is a temporary condition; being poor is a state of mind.

✓ If you live right, things go right.

✓ Good things happen, the harder you work. Great things happen, the smarter you work.

✓ A golden opportunity is often disguised as an impossible situation.

✓ Anything worth doing is worth doing right.

✓ The best thing about the future is that we only receive it one day at a time.

✓ I believe life will eventually give us what we give it, don't you?

✓ Life is the test, not the reward.

✓ Today is your day to climb to the top of the mountain.

✓ It is your attitude and not your aptitude that determines your altitude.

✓ Be willing to ask for help! It will divide your problem—and it will double your joy.

✓ Failure is the path of least persistence.

✓ Success brings with it the challenge to keep moving.

✓ Out of every negative comes a positive.

✓ In one minute I changed my attitude, and in that minute I changed my whole day.

✓ Aim high. There is plenty of room.

✓ Big dreams have the power to move mountains.

✓ From broken dreams new dreams are born.

✓ Luck happens when preparation meets opportunity.

✓ The road to excellence is always under construction.

✓ Success is the progressive realization of goals.

✓ Ethics are what you are in the dark.

✓ Never look behind you because someone may be gaining.

✓ Persistence and determination are omnipotent.

✓ Belief is your life preserver in waters of doubt.

✓ Winners are winners because they win. There's no more to it than that.

✓ Eleven ways to grow a big soul and a big life are: pray big, think big, believe big, act big, dream big, work big, give big, forgive big, love big, live big, laugh big.

✓ Excellence today is not a guarantee of excellence tomorrow.

✓ We seek excellence, and we will go on seeking it because of what we are, why we are, and who we are.

✓ The key to goal setting is to dream big dreams.

✓ Destiny isn't a matter of chance—it's a matter of choice.

✓ Pray to God, but make sure you row toward shore.

✓ The difference between ordinary and extraordinary is that little "extra."

✓ Tradition was meant to be a rudder, not an anchor.

✓ The sands of time are bleached with the bones of those who, on the brink of important decisions, chose to wait until tomorrow.

✓ Any fish can go downstream, but it takes a live fish to go up-stream.

✓ It's time to pull out our old dreams, dust them off, polish them up, and let them guide us through today and tomorrow.

✓ There is no limit to what we can accomplish if it doesn't matter who gets the credit.

✓ It wasn't raining the day Noah built the ark.

✓ I feel good about me when I'm with you.

✓ Expect and accept that we fail more frequently than we succeed.

✓ No guts, no glory.

✓ You can't take somebody to the top of the mountain without getting there yourself.

✓ Problems are those terrifying realities we fear when we take our eyes off our objective.

✓ Failure is not fatal and success is not final.

✓ Don't let the fear of failure keep you from the stimulation of success.

✓ Fear of failure looms as the most insidious challenge to your success.

✓ The greatest richness you can mine are inside you.

✓ Yesterday's luxuries are today's necessities.

✓ Really successful people all seem to have one thing in common: They expect more good out of life than bad. They expect to succeed more often than they expect to fail.

✓ The platinum rule: Do and say unto others what they would like you to do and say unto them.

✓ If you feel you won't be able to win, make sure the one in front of you breaks the record.

✓ A lie will run out—the truth will work out.

✓ It was always my dream to do what I wanted to do, when I wanted to do it, with people of my choice.

✓ Today is a part of eternity.

✓ Get your mind set in the groove it should follow.

✓ Fill up the back of the shovel; the front fills itself up.

✓ You own and control your own thought factory. Each day, you can produce positive or negative thoughts.

✓ Don't be afraid to take a chance with a new idea.

✓ Success is a journey, not a destination.

✓ If you don't believe in yourself, that will probably make it unanimous.

✓ The people who succeed in this world are the people who get up and find the circumstances they want—and if they can't find them, they make them.

✓ Honest, intelligent effort is always rewarded.

✓ Our accomplishments are never less than our belief.

✓ I would rather attempt something great and fail than attempt nothing and succeed.

✓ Don't hesitate to be different and take a new path toward your goal.

✓ The difference between a big shot and a little shot is that the big shot was once a little shot who never stopped shooting.

✓ Work as hard for yourself as you would work for someone else.

✓ There are lots of new ways of looking at old ideas.

✓ The winners played the game and stuck with it. The losers never tried.

✓ Great minds have purposes, others have wishes.

✓ Anytime you can input positive thought into a negative receiver, you're going to short-circuit self-pity.

✓ Successes do not last forever—neither do failures.

✓ The secret in life is learning how to hit the curve ball, not waiting for life to stop throwing curve balls.

✓ If you don't know where you are going, you will end up someplace else.

✓ In my personal life, I need to know where I've been, where I want to go, and why.

✓ I may not be able to control an event, but I can control how I react to that event.

✓ I believe in learning from all my experiences—both successes and failures.

✓ Risking is the normal state of affairs in all development.

✓ The stress encountered while engaging in any kind of risk activity represents a new beginning.

✓ It is better to be sad and wealthy than to be sad and poor.

✓ Money is not a problem until I believe it will solve my problems.

✓ What you are is God's gift to you. What you become is your gift to God.

✓ As Eleanor Roosevelt said, "No one can make you feel inferior without your consent."

✓ Try your best to be as good as your children think you are.

✓ Get down on your knees and pray, then get up and hustle.

✓ You can lead no further than you've been.

✓ I can't afford to spend one minute on negative thinking because that deprives me of one minute of positive thinking.

✓ Never try to teach a pig to sing. It wastes your time and it annoys the pig.

✓ Learn what motivates you, and work hard at it.

✓ Plan for the worst—hope for the best.

✓ A goal is a dream with a deadline.

✓ The road to excellence is always under construction.

✓ When you wake up each morning, the score is nothing to nothing, so start scoring points.

✓ Winning is never final—losing is never fatal.

✓ Be willing to be different.

✓ There is a time for planting and a time for harvesting, and I am in the harvesting season.

✓ Don't worry about the mule going blind. Just load the wagon.

✓ When things go wrong, push harder.

✓ Plan each day as if it were your last. Work each day as if it were your best. Live each day as if it were your first.

✓ In order to be a leader, a person must have a following. The following must be voluntary, and the leader must be able to show his or her followers the best method of getting what they want.

✓ Are you the stuff that dreams are made of?

✓ If you don't know where you're going, you're not likely to get anywhere.

✓ Our success is not dependent on others, so take it upon yourself to do the things necessary to succeed.

✓ Each day, your goal should be to do only what you do best.

✓ Listen to advice and accept instruction, and in the end you will be wise.

✓ An obstacle is what you see when you take your eyes off your goal.

✓ If you plan for success, you will be forming the habits that automatically make you successful.

✓ You are going to make something happen today, and it is going to be fun.

✓ Too many people mistake the ladder of success as an escalator and get on for the ride.

✓ A quick reaction leads to a quick success.

✓ There is no vacation for character.

✓ Potential doesn't mean anything. Developing potential is the key. Most failures have great potential, and die with great potential.

✓ When I hit bottom, I realize that it is the bottom and that is why I'm going up.

✓ At the end of the day, judge your performance by what you have achieved—not what you have left undone.

✓ Enthusiasm is the most contagious commodity on earth.

✓ Nothing can ever be accomplished without enthusiasm.

✓ Being negative is a down payment on failure.

✓ Common sense is not always common.

✓ As long as you're not satisfied with your past, you have a bright future.

✓ I don't always have to be *the* best, but I do have to be *my* best.

✓ Life pays us the income we ask for.

✓ You are a failure only when you quit trying.

✓ Give yourself the courage to meet the valley days when they come.

✓ Misfortunes always come in by the door that has been left open for them.

✓ The penalty of coasting is the bitter ashes of regret.

✓ Don't measure yourself by what you have accomplished, but by what you should have accomplished with your ability.

✓ You are only tired when you lose—not when you win.

✓ To look at something is one thing, but to really see it is all that matters.

✓ Act as though it were impossible to fail, and remember that the only time you fail is the last time you try.

✓ Success comes not from being best but by doing your best.

✓ What keeps me going is the feeling of doing something better today than yesterday.

✓ Unless you know where to go, only a miracle could take you there.

✓ Be careful of what you ask for, because you will surely get it.

✓ Your opportunity to be successful will not change.

✓ In a great attempt, it is glorious even to fail—nobody boos a pole-vaulter who misses at 20 feet.

✓ Always stay in over your head.

✓ If you want to hit the mark, you need to know where the target is.

✓ Sell a prospect. Educate a customer.

✓ Excellence is an art won by training and habituation.

✓ Failure happens to those who thought they worked hard, but didn't.

✓ Failure is the path of least persistence.

✓ Forming the habit of doing things that failures don't like to do is the common denominator of success.

✓ Get your personal affairs and your business affairs under firm control. The best-organized person has the best chance to be a leader.

✓ God gave us two ends—one to sit on and one to think with. Success depends on the end that is used most often.

✓ Good luck results when preparation and opportunity come together.

✓ Half of being smart is knowing what you are dumb at.

✓ Hard work and stress never killed anyone, but fear and worry can
destroy you.

✓ Honest effort is never wasted.

✓ I belong to that group of people who, when challenged, work
harder. Under pressure, we perform better.

✓ If you work hard, the results are easy. If you work easy, the results
are hard.

✓ I have always maintained that my big sales are made at my desk,
not in front of my prospect.

✓ I start each day with a list of things to do, starting with the most
important item.

✓ Ideas are useless unless we attempt to put them into action.

✓ Ideas never work unless you do.

✓ If you always do what you've always done, you'll always get what
you always got.

✓ If you are beginning to encounter some hard bumps, be glad. At
least you are out of the rut.

✓ If you didn't sell anything today, you were unemployed, and you
might as well have stayed home in bed.

✓ If you do something for 37 days in a row, it becomes a habit. It is
then harder not to do it on the 38th day than it is to do it. Try it!

✓ If you don't prepare for change, you'll never be prepared for the
future.

✓ If you want to leave footprints in the sands of time, wear work
shoes.

✓ Improve your effectiveness as a businessperson.

✓ In our business, you earn what you earn.

✓ It is easier to learn how to earn more than to learn how to live on
less.

✓ If it is to be, it is up to me.

✓ It sure is hard to laugh and love unless you are making a living.

✓ It takes years to become a star overnight.

✓ It's amazing how great my attitude is when I'm booked two weeks
in advance and all I have to do is what I do best: tell my story.

✓ Just wanting to be a success won't get you far.

✓ Keep your office door shut. You can get a lot of work done in an
hour with no interruptions.

✓ Look at your desk; stop, think. What is the most productive item on your desk that you can do?

✓ Luck is preparation meeting opportunity.

✓ Luck is: planning, preparation, organized circulation, product knowledge, hard work.

✓ Many events are beyond my control, but how I react to them is within my control.

✓ Many great things are left undone because someone wanted to think about them rather than do them.

✓ Many of us limit our effectiveness by our acceptance of, and indulgence in, the negative.

✓ Many of us need to double our productive activity.

✓ Natural abilities are like natural resources: They must be worked if they are to produce!

✓ Never underestimate the value of a small amount of organized activity.

✓ Nine magic words: Do, Do, Do. When? When? When? Now, Now, Now.

✓ No one has ever drowned in a pool of sweat.

✓ Nothing can replace a system that keeps me on track for timely contact with my clients and prospects.

✓ Nothing is work, unless you'd rather be doing something else.

✓ Number of attempts x percentage of efficiency x average-sized sales = production.

✓ Offer a solution instead of a complaint.

✓ One day a week, leave your comfort zone and go into an untried area.

✓ Only do those things that have to be done as well as only you can do them.

✓ Organize or agonize.

✓ Practice improves most everything—except when we continue to practice our existing work habits!

✓ Prescription for a sales slump: Take two hours of quiet time and review goals and objectives.

✓ Self-discipline married to ordinary ability produces success. Outstanding talent married to self-discipline produces giants!

✓ Sheer persistence is the difference between success and failure.

✓ Slow starters seldom succeed.

✓ Some people do nothing wrong. The problem is, they do nothing and that is what's wrong.

✓ Success is where preparation meets opportunity. Few recognize it because it often comes disguised as hard work.

✓ Success comes to those who hustle while they wait.

✓ Success may be measured in years, but it is accomplished one day at a time.

✓ Successful people are not without problems—they merely are people who have learned how to solve their problems.

✓ The best substitute for genius is persistence.

✓ The bottom line is: Do it!

✓ The first time you touch a piece of paper, you make money; the second time you touch it, you lose money. Minimize your paperwork.

✓ The five most important words are: You did a good job.

✓ The greats in any field never made the grade on a seven-hour day. It hasn't happened in the past and it won't happen in the future.

✓ The harder I work, the luckier I get.

✓ The job rewards people proportionately to what they do—you reap what you sow.

✓ The main thing about this business is establishing work habits and keeping them.

✓ The mistakes I have made because of hasty action are not as great as the opportunities lost because of prolonged thinking.

✓ The more you do, the more you can do!

✓ The only place success precedes work is in the dictionary.

✓ The person who combines raw talent with an enormous capacity for work usually wins.

✓ The person who says it cannot be done should not interrupt the person doing it.

✓ The price of success is hard, intelligent work. The price of failure is worry, dissatisfaction, loss of self-esteem, and a shortage of income. Whether you succeed or fail, the cost will be high.

✓ The reason worry kills more people than work is that more people worry than work.

✓ The root of all paperwork is called reluctance.

✓ The secrets of success do not work unless you do.

✓ The successful keep score. They record not only the results but, more importantly, their activities.

✓ There is no easy way out. I have to work to make a living.

✓ There is no such thing as being lucky, you make your own breaks.

✓ There is nothing so fatiguing as the eternal hanging-on of an un-completed task.

✓ Today's preparation determines tomorrow's achievement.

✓ We are what we repeatedly do. Excellence, then, is not an act, but a habit.

✓ We first make our habits and then our habits make us.

✓ When the phone rings, I know when to say "No" and how to say "No."

✓ When there's a breakdown, when things go wrong, if you look in the mirror you can usually find the person responsible for it.

✓ When you lose your temper, you lose.

✓ Which one of these people is more dependable? Why does that person do so well?

✓ Work will work, when wishy-washy wishing won't.

✓ Worry is never productive.

✓ Worrying is stewing and not doing.

✓ Write it. Definiteness ends confusion.

✓ You don't make right decisions—you make decisions, then make them right.

✓ You either make dust, or you eat dust.

✓ You manage things—you lead people.

✓ You will get out of your day what you put in.

✓ Normally, you don't just kill time, you murder success.

✓ We need to ask ourselves, with each project we face, "Is this the best possible use of my time, based on my priorities and objectives?"

✓ Planning is important. If you do not know where you're going, you may not get there.

✓ An agent's only real competition is the first 40 hours every week.

✓ Time is the greatest problem in stress.

✓ A time-control schedule is like the rudder on a ship.

✓ Time management is the art of identifying, delegating, and performing those tasks that will produce the maximum results for the time invested.

✓ Procrastination is synonymous with neglect.

✓ I can do anything, but only one thing at a time.

✓ Everything we do in life falls into categories that are 85 percent routine and 15 percent innovative. But there is no law that says we have to spend 85 percent of our time on routine matters.

✓ You do the best with the moments you can control, which is now.

✓ Too often, timing has become confused with procrastination!

✓ I spend three to fours hours each week planning. The process is never-ending, but rewarding.

✓ No great task was ever accomplished that did not begin with a plan.

✓ Measure twice, cut once.

✓ Be "yield conscious" with your time. Invest time capital like money capital. Examine your ROTA (Return on Time Allocation) daily!

✓ Do you spend less than 20 percent of your time face-to-face with clients?

✓ Plans without actions are like architects without contractors.

✓ Only the future is significant.

✓ Time waits for no one, so do it now.

✓ Plan your work, work your plan.

✓ First things first, second things never.

✓ Today is the tomorrow you worried about yesterday.

✓ Time management is the key outside function of success.

✓ Most people don't plan to fail, they fail to plan.

✓ Are you a doer or a plan-to-doer?

✓ Every day, we're poured a cupful of time. You either drink yours or spill it on the floor.

✓ Great plans only come from great planning.

✓ Everybody gets 24 hours a day—how you use yours makes you successful.

✓ I spend one or two hours in the planning process each Sunday evening. I put down on paper everything I want to do the next week.

✓ Consumers still want to talk to and work with people who care about them as individuals.

✓ Get a savings commitment from a prospect, regardless of the length of the commitment.

✓ Get your prospects off your to-do list and into your appointment book.

✓ Have you made a sale today? If not, why not?

✓ I can talk to someone on the phone and hear in his or her voice whether or not I'll make a sale.

✓ I need your help.

✓ If no new business is done within five years, that customer is dropped from my follow-up system.

✓ If there is a sense of urgency, the client will buy.

✓ If your client knows why he or she is buying the product, he or she will pay anything to get it.

✓ If your concern is how to benefit your client, the commission falls into place.

✓ Knowledge and calls are the keys to success in business.

✓ Mr./Mrs. Prospect, when all is said and done, more is said than done.

✓ Mr./Mrs. Prospect, are you aware that over 90 percent of your assets are standing in your shoes?

✓ Mr./Mrs. Prospect, may we talk, just to see if we really should talk?

✓ My rough definition of a client is someone who buys from me most of the time.

✓ Prospecting and service are the keys to a successful selling career.

✓ Sometimes I see people weighing all the pros and cons so long it seems they are never going to make a decision.

✓ Success or greatness is a matter of small numbers—one more telephone call, one more appointment, one more time through the proposal.

✓ When a client calls with a problem, he or she is really calling with an unresolved opportunity.

✓ You cannot ask for more from the prospect than the prospect asks from himself or herself.

✓ You cannot even give your product away, unless there is a perceived need.

✓ Most of my clients have traditional values, and so do I. This helps me solve their problems.

✓ Ask the prospect to buy!

✓ A lot of publicity is not the same as good publicity.

✓ Honesty is not the best policy; it is the only policy.

✓ If they know I'm in the business, they'll come to me when they're ready.

✓ If we always speak the truth, we will never have to be concerned with our memory.

✓ It is amazing how valuable a few kind words are.

✓ Love your clients and they will love you.

✓ Make promises sparingly and keep them faithfully.

✓ Never destroy—you don't strengthen the weak by weakening the strong.

✓ Pass the praise.

✓ People don't care how much you know until they know how much you care.

✓ Public relations is performance plus recognition.

✓ Tell people the truth. Then you don't have to worry about anything.

✓ Tell the truth and you never need to keep a record of it.

✓ The successful sales professional is a public relations expert.

✓ Trust is the only reason one person will do business with another.

✓ Wear a smile—it increases your face value, and one size fits all.

✓ A great deal of success with referred leads depends on how well and how quickly you follow up.

✓ A "No" today is not a "No" forever.

✓ A professional becomes referable. Instead of relying on referrals, be referable.

✓ A prospect is a client who has not yet bought from you.

✓ All of the good ideas of the past and present aren't any good if you don't have anybody to talk to.

✓ An application a day keeps the creditors away!

✓ Be prepared for 1 in 10.

✓ Call someone new each day.

✓ Do you feel you are doing more for your client than he or she is doing for you with the recent sale?

✓ Don't look for prospects—look for problems.

✓ Everyone in the office helps to get appointments for me.

✓ Everyone is a prospect.

✓ Focus on potential clients, and then determine who can make an introduction.

✓ For referrals, don't forget the four most beautiful words in the English language: I need your help.

✓ Go to them. If they don't know you, they cannot come to you.

✓ "Guaranteed": 100 percent of the people you don't ask to buy, don't buy from you.

✓ I consider my clients to be my friends.

✓ I get paid in two ways, Mr./Ms. Prospect. If I've done a good job, give me my second payment—a referral.

✓ If new sales professionals could realize that prospects aren't rejecting them personally, there would be fewer failures among them.

✓ If you see enough people, you're going to sell your product.

✓ If you want referrals from businesspeople, ask them who their chief suppliers are.

✓ It takes 10 "No's" to get one "Yes."

✓ It's the number of clients you have that determines your income.

✓ I've never been able to equal the results I get with referred leads.

✓ Just be yourself and ask the people. They're not going to bite you!

✓ Lions fail in the hunting 80 percent of the time, but they come back to hunt again.

✓ Make the call!

✓ My satisfied clients and their referrals provide 68 percent of my business year in and year out.

✓ No sales professional ever failed because he or she had too many appointments.

✓ "No" is always the answer if you don't ask the question.

✓ No matter how good you and your product are, if you don't have anyone to tell your story to, you're out of business.

✓ No matter what happens, somebody is always making money. Figure out who those people are and call on them.

✓ Nothing happens until you pick up the phone.

✓ Older prospects understand their problems more readily. They can see their needs more easily.

✓ One hundred percent of our sales come from existing clients. In many cases, they were other people's existing clients.

✓ Your job is to find people with money and grow with them.

✓ People like to do business with people they know or know of. What better reason is there to ask for referrals?

✓ Prospect well and you won't have to sell.

✓ Prospecting—the heart and soul of selling—requires you to move from your comfort zone into your action zone.

✓ Prospecting and selling are like shaving—if you don't do it every day, you end up a bum!

✓ Prospecting is far more important than closing in determining success in our business.

✓ Prospecting is like peeling potatoes—take the big with the small, but just keep peeling.

✓ Prospecting is simply people plus a good idea.

✓ Regardless of your commitments, ask at least one person every day to buy your product or service.

✓ Remember, you have done a good job. You have the right to be recommended.

✓ See the people! See the people! See the people!

✓ Set a goal for the next 30 days. Break it apart. Make a list of 10 names for your first week, and you're on your way.

✓ Stress is not having enough prospects. Pressure is not having enough time to see the prospects you have.

✓ Successful selling is the art of finding buyers.

✓ Systematic client upgrading—ask your top 50 clients for only one referral.

✓ The best informed, strongest sales professional in the world can't sell to a poor prospect. The worst sales professional often sells to a good prospect.

✓ The client pays and the prospect doesn't.

✓ The clients you work with can speak so loudly for you that nothing else will be necessary.

✓ The guy you don't call on don't buy nothin'.

✓ The hard work is in finding the name in the first place. So I am not going to throw out a name just because the prospect says "No" the first time.

✓ The most highly trained sales professional with no prospects is like the Concorde with no fuel—neither has the energy to get off the ground.

✓ The most successful sales professionals are the ones who hear "No" the most.

✓ The phone does not weigh 300 pounds. Lift it and make those prospecting phone calls.

✓ The problem really isn't finding the prospects. They are all around us. Approaching them is the problem.

✓ The prospect list is the lifeblood of our business. When people say "No," they don't mean they'll never buy from you. They mean, "No, not now."

✓ The three secrets of success in the sales business: See the people, See the people, See the people.

✓ There are only two kinds of sales—the easy one and the one you don't get.

✓ There are too many good prospects to waste my time on poor ones.

✓ Turn prospecting into a procedure so that it no longer becomes a problem.

✓ We need to become conscious of the client's environment so that we can easily become part of his or her world.

✓ When you ask for a referral, what you are asking is, "Will you help me?"

✓ You are told what is important is the people you know. I say the important thing is the people who know you.

✓ You can do a lot of business by accident if you get out there where the accidents are happening.

✓ You can see that the work I do for a client is extensive and time-consuming. To be of greater service to my clients, I have to rely on them to refer me to their friends who might find this complete service helpful.

✓ You can't plough a field by turning it over in your mind.

CONCLUSION

B y now, the definition of closing should be clear: It is *anything* that sales professionals put into selling that causes prospects to make a purchasing decision. *Everything* might be a better word, for closing is not so much a separate step in the selling process as it is the result of all steps that sales professionals must take in order to complete sales.

You have learned that the significant difference between successful and unsuccessful sales professionals is not found so much in the effort applied or the knowledge of what their products or services do; rather, the difference is measured by the sales professionals' own attitudes. The depth and strength of their conviction are akin to ownership of the products and services sold, and they offer the best and often the only solutions to the specific problems of prospects. To gain and hold this conviction, sales professionals must know, definitely and uncontrovertibly, exactly why it is vitally important to prospects to buy *now*.

When this knowledge resides in sales professionals' attitudes, when this conviction is solidly founded on a real understanding of prospects' actual situations, and when it is sincere and unshakable, the close represents no insurmountable obstacles. However, no one should have the impression that even the most successful MDRT sales professional will always find closing easy. It is not.

Prospects are people, and most people reach decisions reluctantly. The decision to buy your products and service—and to buy them now—is apt to be unusually difficult for many prospects. Sales professionals are people, too. And most sales professionals are as reluctant to direct their prospects' decisions as their prospects are to make decisions.

Closing can be difficult for some sales professionals. Following are a few of the important reasons for reluctance to attempt to close. Sales professionals:

- ✓ Are afraid that prospects will turn them down.
- ✓ Are not convinced that their product is the right one for the prospect.
- ✓ See closing as a separate step, not as an integrated and continuous part of the sales process.
- ✓ Are unable to handle prospects' objections.

The close begins the minute sales professionals and prospects meet, and it should flow easily throughout the entire sales presentation. Good closers make it easy for prospects to agree to the sale. They give the prospect a chance to buy; they don't talk past the point of the sale; they recognize a genuine closing opportunity. Good closers are persistent; they know why they are there. In addition, they have accepted the responsibility for directing their prospects' decisions—even to the extent of making them, when they know a decision is vital and when directing it is not enough to close the sale.

This book has presented a variety of closing methodologies and techniques that should make you a good closer. Once you have achieved this rank, your sales success will gain unlimited potential—the potential that typifies the sales success of the Million Dollar Round Table membership.

A FINAL NOTE

The books in this series are based on the experience of some of the top salespeople in the world. The secrets and techniques they provide will help you to prospect, close, and sell more effectively and efficiently, and improving these skills will improve your sales ratio and thus your career. You would not have purchased this book if you were not motivated by success, but does a greater volume of sales make you successful? All of the salespeople who contributed to this book would say that sales volume leads to success, but does not define it. In fact, all of the most successful salespeople in the Million Dollar Round Table are firm adherents to the association's Whole Person Philosophy, which maintains that to meet one's highest professional potential, one must strive to meet the highest potential in all other parts of life.

A whole person is committed to a life of significance, happiness and fulfillment and understands that leading such a life requires a continual process of growth. Success in any area of life, be it familial, health, educational, career, service, financial, or spiritual, is dependent upon success in and balance with the other areas since all areas of life are intertwined.

Sales is a career that demands extraordinary dedication. The hours are arduous, the reactions of prospects can be hostile or humiliating, and the financial rewards are variable. After a long day cold calling or meeting with uncooperative prospects, it can be difficult to spend time and energy on your family, on caring for your body, or on the pursuit of further education. It is not always easy to comprehend that good health, good family relationships, and a commitment to education will enhance your sales career, but the experience of thousands of MDRT members has proved this true. When you are confident, when you are healthy, when you live by a secure code of values, and when you are able to adapt to change, you will inspire the respect and trust of your prospects, and sales will follow.

From the very beginning, a successful salesperson must demonstrate responsibility. The high producing salesperson practices responsibility to prospects, in providing them with the best product to meet their needs and their budget. In addition, a successful salesperson must be responsible to herself, in putting forth the time and effort to do the prospecting that must be done to get appointments and to be successful. An expert salesperson is also responsible to his industry, educating himself and using good moral judgment to improve the public's preconceptions about salespeople, and responsible to his community, giving time, energy, and money back to the area that provides his clients and therefore his living.

For some, the responsibilities of sales are overwhelming to the point they are ignored, which is why many sales careers are so brief. For others, the responsibility of gathering and maintaining a client base can be so wearing that other areas of responsibility become subordinate. Persistence in sales can be as dangerous as giving up if the salesperson is focused on aspects of the career that won't lead to success. Often, the highest producers spend less time at work than those who are struggling even to obtain interviews. It is difficult to know when to draw the line between a persistent person and a workaholic, and, as one MDRT member points out, frequently the training for a sales career convinces new salespeople that workaholic is synonymous with success. As he says:

> The [sales] business is a unique and curious business. We are attracted to this great business because of the opportunities and the unlimited possibilities. And truly, they are unlimited. I do not know of any other occupation where the average person, equipped with desire, motivation, and discipline, can achieve an elite standard of living and still be helping others. The successes of this business are paradoxical. The personal sacrifices and undaunted discipline needed to make it in this great business are also the traits that so often turn one into a workaholic.
>
> In the [sales] business, we, our careers, our measures as human beings in the business world, are measured by the amount of money we are able to make. In fact, in this business, our ranking as individuals is based on the amount of production we do month in and month out-and on into years. Early in my career, I had been brainwashed in the same way, and consequently money and money-oriented goals became the number one priority in my life. Now I know, in order to become a truly happy and successful individual, and salesperson, one must write down one's goals, love and serve people, and work.

Isolating oneself as a workaholic will not increase sales in the long term. Instead, concentrating on changing one's perceptions about oneself, and developing and growing in all areas of life will permanently increase your ability to gain sales. For too long the sales profession has defined success in terms of monetary goals. The Whole Person Philosophy is designed to help you meet those goals while focusing on how to develop a successful life, not just a successful production year.

Career

A successful career is based upon four major components: discipline, vision, goals, and ethics. To become a great salesperson, one must concentrate on all four. To do this, as one MDRT producer insists, you must make a committed decision to be abnormal. Most people spend the majority of their lives striving to be normal—to fit comfortably within their community, their office, their group of friends. Why the sudden need to become different, to become other than what your peers are, to become abnormal? Because the normal people, the majority, are the status quo, who are mired in routine. To be a success, you need to be able to think outside the box, to question the routines and procedures that have always been followed "because they work," and alter them so they work even better. Unless you make a commitment to excel in your life and your business, you will be among the 80 percent who are normal, and normal is, at best, average, and, at worst, mediocre. To be a success you must be able to leave behind the comfort of rut and routine, and join the abnormal—the 20 percent minority of the population that is exploring and experimenting to create progress.

To leave the majority behind requires a tremendous amount of discipline. First, it requires the discipline to do what is difficult rather than what comes naturally: to analyze your actions and determine what works, rather than following the generally accepted procedure. Second, it requires the discipline to push outside your comfort zone in order to reach new levels of success when you are already successful. Third, it requires the discipline to realize no job is too small to be done to the best of your ability. In short, discipline is the difference between success and mediocrity. As a top producer in MDRT relates, "Successful people discipline themselves to do the things the less successful don't like to do." He continues:

Successful people understand it isn't the big jobs which bring success. It's the little things we have to do every day. What will surprise you here is there are no extraordinary people, but some have disciplined themselves to achieve extraordinary goals. Discipline not to go home on a Friday until the diary is full for the following week. Discipline to break down the goals into daily tasks. What do I have to do now, today, which if I repeat it day after day, will bring my goals to reality? It's what we do each day that determines our failure or success. Success is something we have to practice on a daily basis.

The discipline to become successful has to be rewarded by something, or it would be simpler to continue doing things as you have always done them. All discipline results from a vision. Those salespeople who have the discipline to make success happen a little at a time derive that discipline from seeing themselves as successful. Most people want to improve their lives and careers, in other words, most people want to be successful. In spite of this, most people are unable to discipline themselves to think and act differently, because they are unable to envision themselves as successful. A respected member of MDRT explains the importance of vision this way:

> People of greatness don't get there by accident. The person who gets to the top of the mountain didn't fall there! They become masterful by making choices and decisions of exactly what it is they want to achieve. When you realize that the world we live in is entirely made up, then you are free to create the world you want. All of us know that goals sculpt and shape our lives. We know that, we've heard about their importance enough times haven't we? However, goals alone are not enough to turn your life into a masterpiece.
>
> Many people make the mistake of just setting goals without having something greater to live for, without a deep felt

purpose at the core of your very being. As George Bernard Shaw wrote, "A purpose recognized by yourself is a mighty one." We need to go beyond goal setting, because goal setting on its own has limitations.

Everything large is built up from small pieces; giant leaps are the accumulation of many smaller leaps. Realization of your vision doesn't come usually in one move, but one step at a time. The whole is the sum total of its parts. What's important is that each smaller step is a part of the big picture, otherwise you can still be a goal achiever, and not be a success.

Think of your vision as a jigsaw puzzle. It can't be done in one move, or by rushing and jamming pieces into place. The only way is by visualizing the finished image and then working piece by piece, day by day. Then what happens is as you begin to solve it the quicker and easier you complete it. You build momentum. If you build a little on a little and do this often, soon it becomes big. Without a vision the goals will not take the shape of the whole, will they?

Your daily actions and activities should come not only from your goals, but from your vision. This will give your daily activities more meaning and purpose.

Your vision of yourself provides you the motivation to complete the daily tasks that are inherent in being a successful salesperson. Goals are the way you can measure progress in reaching your vision, and the way you can focus your discipline to directly lead from where you are to where you envision yourself. As one motivational expert at an MDRT meeting said, "goals manipulate process." Achievement of your vision is dependent upon practical application of the discipline your vision has instilled in you, and goals allow you to apply that discipline.

A goal is a piece of the jigsaw puzzle that composes your vision. With each goal you meet, you are getting closer to the success you envision yourself to be, and each goal you meet makes subsequent goals easier because of the confidence attaining goals lends you. For a goal to assist you in becoming your vision, it must be realistic. It is best to start with smaller goals, such as "I will call twenty new prospects every day next week," and build up to goals like "I will be my business' highest producer this year," or the system will backfire. By setting unrealistic goals you are procrastinating on reaching your vision, since each goal that you fail to meet will make you less likely to move forward. This is not to say your goals should be things you know you can do. As one well-known motivation researcher states, goals are most effective if they have a 50 percent chance of failure:

> What research has discovered, and what could be pure gold for anyone who understood how to apply it, is that your goals will continue to strengthen your motivation up to the fifty percent probability of success. In other words, your goals are most motivating, they tap into your most powerful inner resources, when you have a 50/50 chance at reaching them, when your probability of success is fifty percent. And no motivation is aroused when the goal is perceived as being either virtually certain, or virtually impossible to attain. This provides the answer for so many sales professionals who seem to lose their achievement drive. They have failed to use goals to fuel their internal fire, to motivate themselves properly.

Goals are motivation to maintain the discipline that is used to fuel the conversion of your vision into a reality. Every time you reach a goal you are propelled to achieve more, because you have the confidence of achievement and because you have a new habit for success. According to recent research, it takes 21 days to establish a new habit. When you raise the bar to reach a goal, and are doing something every day to ensure your success, after 21 days it becomes second nature—a part of your established routine. So, even after your goal has been met, you will be in the habit of doing something that has contributed to your success. Many people focus on the end, the meeting of a goal, as the main benefit, but the adoption of habits that allow you to reach the goal are every bit as important. As many MDRT members have pointed out, success is a process, not an event. The habits you develop in pursuit of a goal will make you more successful, as will the attitude you develop from the implementation of those habits. A top member and motivational expert said:

> Ongoing action supports a goal. And whenever we are in action towards a goal, we feel better about ourselves, our energy is higher, our confidence and self-esteem are growing in strength. When we coast, when our achievement drive is low, our self-esteem goes down, we retreat into our comfort zones, and lose much of our enthusiasm for life. Our attitude goes sour.

Goals are important because they improve your habits and they alter your attitude. When we are efficient and we are full of energy we are more capable of success, and the more successful we are in reaching our goals, the easier it becomes for us to set more.

While determining visions, setting goals, and using discipline to reach them, one must be certain that the vision of success is based on solid ethical principles. Becoming a success takes a great deal of work and energy, and any path to success that does not include hard work and effort is bound to be faulty. As one member of MDRT says, "doing the right thing goes hand in hand with doing well. There are ways to become successful with no great investment of time and energy, but the success you will attain using these methods will be transparent and transitory." The only way to be successful is to inspire your prospects to believe in you, and this will only happen if they can see you creating successful habits and meeting goals. Instant success is possible through only the most unethical methods, that initially hurt others, but eventually will hurt the people who practice them.

Sales is a profession that is frequently accused of questionable ethics. We have all seen films or heard jokes that feature unscrupulous used car dealers, or salespeople who are thinly disguised con men. These negative stereotypes make it all the more important that your sales dealings be straightforward and honest ones. To find and keep customers you need to take personal responsibility for who you are and what you do. When your prospects see that you are someone focused on success and working hard to get there, they will feel comfortable giving you their business. When they see how your goal-oriented habits and discipline are put to work in their best interests, they will become clients, giving you more business, referring you to their friends, and contributing to your success.

This can be a slow process, and at times it will be tempting to place immediate success over honesty, integrity, and fairness. If you are to be successful in sales, you will be patient, and put in the hours and work rather than pursue personal gain through shady business dealings. A past president of MDRT told this story to emphasize how important ethics are to success:

> I think that sometimes nice guys may appear to finish last, but that's because they're running in a different race. For example, Australian golfer, Greg Norman, is one of the biggest draws on the pro tour. He was among the leaders of the 1996 Greater Hartford open, when he disqualified himself by reporting to tournament officials that he had inadvertently played with an improper ball for the first two rounds. That's ethics. There is no pillow as soft—or as comforting—as a clear conscience.

Questionable ethics may allow you to win sales in the short term, but long-term success is conditional upon loyal clients, who will only come to you when, like Norman, you admit your wrongs and prove your commitment to ethical business dealings.

To have a successful sales career you must be able to envision yourself as a success. Then, you must break your vision into smaller goals, and develop the habits and the discipline to meet them. You must live by a code of ethics that insists upon honesty, fairness, compassion, and hard work, and the sales will follow.

Education

Education is closely related to the area of sales success. Your vision of sales success can be broken down into goals, like completing professional training or designation programs, that will increase customer confidence and therefore sales, but education is an area of life distinct from either career or play.

As the inspiration for the Whole Person Philosophy, Dr. Mortimer J. Adler, explains, education is part of an important life category known as leisure. Leisure activities are activities that provide no extrinsic gain or compensation, but rather intrinsic rewards. These activities may be extremely grueling, but are worth doing despite the difficulty of the tasks. As we must have work in order to live, we must have leisure in order to live well. Dr. Adler explains:

> Leisure activities either produce a growth in the human person, a development of the self, or they produce advances in civilization, developments in the arts and sciences. Any form of learning, any form of creative work, any form of political or socially useful activity, is a leisure activity. Anything which contributes to the advancement of society is a leisure

activity. It follows, then, that leisure activities are those which are morally obligatory.

As a sales professional you serve the public as a trusted advisor, and are responsible for being up to date with current knowledge and developments in your field in order to serve your clients in the best way possible.

Pursuit of education makes you more confident with prospects, and this, in turn, increases sales. Confidence is rarely achieved through public adulation. Instead, confidence usually comes from competence, which in turn comes from knowledge. When you increase your knowledge and confidence, you become more aware of your values, behave in a more creative manner, communicate things you believe in to others better, and are able to translate ideas into action through consistent hard work. Hard work without a sense of direction leads to frustration, but education can focus your work, increase your confidence, and help you analyze and improve your professional skills. As one MDRT member asserts, our success in becoming a professional human being depends very much on the efforts we make to understand and continue our own professional self-growth and development.

We no longer have the luxury of dying in the same world into which we were born. We are undergoing constant change. A development committee at Sony determined that at the current rate of technological change a new product becomes obsolete every 18 days. To be successful in an environment like this, you need to be able to think of a way to replace that product and get it out before the eighteenth day, so that you aren't surpassed by another company. Many people carry palm pilots. These computers, small enough to fit into a shirt pocket, contain more computer technology than was available in the whole world in 1985. The world we live in demands constant education to meet the demands of its constant change. A highly respected MDRT member sums this up well when he says:

> We need to continually educate and reeducate ourselves so that our knowledge and skills are cutting edge. As business guru Alvin Toffler says, "The illiterates of the future are not those who cannot read and write, but those who cannot learn, unlearn, and relearn."

Charles Darwin says the success of a species has little to do with its size or its strength, but everything to do with its ability to adapt to changing circumstances. The same can be said of the success of a salesperson. As one motivational expert says, "In a post-industrial economy, people aren't a factor of production, people are the competitive edge. If you're not educated, it's not that you will be unimportant to the society. If you are not educated, you will be irrelevant to the society. If you are not educated, you are not working." He goes on to say:

> In a post-industrial society, schools, corporate training programs, and seminars are the farms of the future. People are the new products. You are the new crops. We taught you to believe that education was the pursuit of knowledge. All you wanted was to make an "A" on a test, to graduate on time, or get credit for going to some seminar. But education is not about the pursuit of knowledge, it's about the pursuit of significance. It's about making a difference with your life. It's about adding value to your work and those around you. It is about giving all you can give and maximizing your talents. Knowledge is something you get along the way.

Education and knowledge are important because they change your dealings with other people, especially prospects, for the better, but they are essential because they force you to deal with yourself differently. Sales careers have a tendency to force people to see their success and significance purely in terms of monetary goals, which can become difficult to meet in this era of constant change. It is a comfort to pursue higher education in situations like this, because it relieves you of the pressure inherent in equating money with success. Education does not have to be formal in order to assist you in expanding your vision of success; in fact, one MDRT member feels the education he accomplishes on his own is as helpful as enrollment in any taught program. He advises:

> I memorize one message every month. Memorizing positive statements, poems and things, really helps round out, not only one's mind, but the way one views the world, and I need to start doing more of it. What we memorize is what we become, in part, a product of.

Education forces you to expand your thinking about success and about the world and your place in it. As long as you are learning, you are growing, and growth gives you the confidence and competence you need to be successful in a world of continual change. As a long-term MDRT member says:

> Growth is the only essence of life. It's a sign you are alive. Look around you in nature. Things are either growing or they're dying. There's no in between. In nature nothing retires. The masters know that there's no limit to their growth. The sky is absolutely not the limit! By continuously increasing their skills, they increase their abilities to add value to others. Change is a process, not a destination.

Education will keep your competence, and therefore high-lightyour confidence, at the point it needs to be to help prospects through the constant change today's world thrusts upon us. It will help you to realize how broad the definition of success is, and keep you moving on your quest to become a successful person. The more education you pursue, the more you will achieve as a salesperson, as a member of your community, as a member of your family, and as a human being.

Health

Without good health, all of your efforts in improving your career and improving your mind will come to nothing. The biggest medical buzzword of the past two decades is stress. The complex juggling act modern life has become makes stress increasingly evident in all areas of life. For salespeople, stress can be especially detrimental. In a career with no set income, with long hours, and with daily duties that can be emotionally taxing, it is no wonder that many salespeople are not as attentive to their health as they should be. Although it seems overwhelming and discouraging at the end of a long day, most of the stress we are under is artificially constructed. As a stress expert who addressed MDRT says:

> Consider how far from normal stress your life has gotten. Normal stress goes like this—The sun is up! We need to kill a rabbit or pick some corn or something before that sun goes down. Come on, family, let's go do this together! So as a family you chase the rabbit or pick the corn, and in the process get some sunshine and exercise, roll in the clover, and take a dip in the farm pond. At the end of the day, you all go home and cook what you've caught or harvested, sit in front of the fire, spend time together, go to sleep, wake up the next day and do it again. That's normal stress.

The stress most of us deal with on a daily basis has nothing to do with this. We have plenty to eat, plenty to wear, and a warm spot to sleep, and in spite of this we work ourselves up about things that truly don't matter. For instance, did I call enough prospects today? Will I have enough appointments this week? Will I sell enough this quarter to take the holiday I want? This stress makes us unable to relax or rest, and lack of rest and relaxation increases our feelings of stress. Many of us use stress to excuse the things we are doing that are actually causing us more stress. Have you ever heard anyone say "Oh, I didn't get a chance to eat dinner last night, I was so busy working on that important policy," or "I know I should quit smoking, but I'm under too much stress for that right now?" The majority of Americans have unhealthy habits that contribute to our stressful lives, but we refuse to alter those habits because of a fear that change will create more stress. Thirty-three percent of Americans smoke. Ten percent of Americans drink too much alcohol. Sixty-seven percent of Americans are not physically active, and 88 percent of Americans have an unhealthy diet. And, if these physical statistics are not shocking enough, look at the financial and emotional consequences of stress. In 1997, an expert in stress told MDRT members:

> The cost of this big life is formidable, for us as individuals in our business, and for us in our intimate relationships. As individuals, the incidence of stress-related illness has increased 800 percent, to the tune of $300 million a year in this country during the past decade. In our business the MERC Family Fund has found that, excluding retirees, over the past five years 28 percent of the American workforce has made voluntary changes that involved making less money, in order to feel that they can balance work and family. In spite of this, 40 to 60 percent of the people who got married yesterday for the first time will be divorced in seven years.
>
> Stress is inevitable, but struggling is optional. If you want to minimize the negative effect of the struggle of stress, you have to take care of your body and maintain caring connections with your colleagues, your community, and an intimate loved one.

Although stress makes us feel there are not enough hours in the day, the only proven way to cure it is to take more time out of the day in order to care for yourself, your family, and your community. It seems like a paradox, but this problem can be resolved with minimal effort on your part. All that is required is a schedule that you will adhere to. No matter how complex your life is, everyone has seven 24-hour days to live in every week, which works out to 168 hours each week. Subtract from these 168 hours the amount of time you require working and sleeping, and you are left with an enormous bank of hours to do with as you like. Now, take this bank of hours, and subtract the amount of time each week it will take you to eat three meals a day and exercise three times a week, and you still have a large amount of time left to spend with your family, on your education, or for relaxation. Though these added commitments may seem to add more stress to your daily routine, they actually will decrease your anxiety if you adhere to them. This commitment to health will enable you to cope with the inescapable stresses of your daily life in a healthy and efficient manner, and introduce you to a method of dealing with stress used by most high-powered professionals; the Three C's of healthy stress. The Three-C method has three simple steps:

1. Viewing stressful situations as Challenges, not problems.
2. Commiting to facing the challenge.
3. Implementing a sense of Control over the coping process.

Acknowledging that your stress is artificial and unnecessary, and making a commitment to be as stress-free as possible through understanding that you are in control of the way your time is spent is a perfect example of using the Three-C method to live a healthier life. And when you are feeling good, chances are the little problems that can develop into stress will be solved before they escalate. You will find that by organizing your time you will accomplish more and be more respected in your career, your education, your community, and your family, and still have time to devote to your health.

Service

In the last speech he ever gave, legendary humanist and Nobel Peace Prize winner Albert Schweitzer said, "I don't know you, but I can tell you that those among you who will be happy are those who have sought and learned how to serve." You have learned that to be successful you must succeed in areas of your life other than your career. You must demonstrate a commitment to pursue education and a conscious attempt to be healthy and happy. Another quality that all successful sales professionals share is a moral obligation to serve their communities. The act of serving others enhances all of the other success habits. It will make you more successful in your career by introducing you to other volunteers who may become clients, and getting your name out in front of people so you receive more customers. It will make you more successful in your education, because you will learn how to apply the skills and ideas you are learning in classes to make life better for other people, and you will undoubtedly learn many important lessons from those you volunteer to help. It will make you more successful in your health because you always feel better about yourself when you are helping others, and it will make you more successful in your family because, through your example, you will be able to teach your children the value of serving others.

Salespeople owe a great debt to their communities, since the people who make up the community are the source of the salesperson's income. Despite this, it is easy for to forget the importance of community obligations. As a renowned MDRT member says:

There's more to life than selling. Almost everyone would like to exercise regularly, diet, and control their weight, to do things that will broaden their minds, to devote more time to continuing an intimate relationship with their spouse, to really get to know their children better on a one-to-one basis, to spend more time with their family, to be active in their religious center of choice, to tackle a worthwhile community problem, and to become more involved in our industry organizations. But many of us fall into a trap of feeling that the sales we make are so socially beneficial to everybody that we don't have time to get involved in any other aspect of our industry or, for that matter, in the other parts of life. But, the more we get involved in religious, community, and association activities the more we achieve a feeling of self-fulfillment.

As a salesperson you are helping people to improve their lives every day while you are at work but, as this MDRT member recognizes, this is not enough. To be truly balanced and successful, it is necessary to spend time giving back to your community in ways not directly related to your career.

Through volunteering, as a life-long volunteer who spoke to MDRT members says: "We find our allies. Our true friends come together to accomplish something. We find our faith, and we discover the power we have to change our lives and the lives of those around us. But finally, we find that to be a true hero is not to ride off into the sunset. The hero must always return to his people, to his community, to make a difference."

It is a very simple thing to volunteer to improve your community. There is an overwhelming number of tasks that must be completed for every community to be a healthy and happy one to live in and there are never enough people to complete these tasks. Churches, schools, hospitals, libraries, political groups, and children's athletic clubs are always in need of volunteers. If none of these places appeal to you, try your local paper to see if volunteers are needed, or contact an organization such as the National Association for Volunteer Administration (P.O. Box 32092, Richmond, VA 23294) to find out about various volunteer opportunities in your community. Some organizations that always need assistance are:

Democratic National Committee
430 S. Capital St. S.E.
Washington, DC 20003
202-863-8000
www.democrats.org

Republican National Committee
310 First St. S.E.
Washington, DC 20003
202-863-8500
www.rnc.org

National Parent Teacher Association
330 N. Wabash Ave.
Suite 2100
Chicago, IL 60611
800-307-4PTA
www.pta.org

International Red Cross
Public Inquiry Office
11th Floor
1621 N. Kent St.
Arlington, VA 22209
703-248-4222
www.redcross.org

Big Brothers/Big Sisters of America
230 N. 13th St.
Philadelphia, PA 19107
215-567-7000
www.bbbsa.org

Contacting the headquarters of these associations will give you information about volunteer opportunities in your area. If you are not already involved in your community, volunteer immediately. Success is sure to follow. As Ralph Waldo Emerson said, "To know that even one life has breathed better because you have lived, this is to have succeeded."

Family

The area in life where it is vital to be a success is with your family. As a respected MDRT member says, "There is no degree of success in the field that is worth failure at home." Your family, when you have a healthy relationship with them, are your greatest motivational force and support system. It is your responsibility to motivate and support them in return. To be a successful family member, you must place your family above the demands of all other people and organizations. Business, education, and play commitments are all secondary to strong relationships with your family members. If nothing else, you must make sure that your family eats at least one meal a day together, sharing and learning from one another. As one expert on family communication told MDRT:

> Other institutions have one by one stripped the family of its former functions. Educating children, giving religious training, supervising health care and providing training for a life's vocation were once the responsibility of families. Today these things are provided by institutions outside the home. The family has become essentially a group of people whose main purpose in being together is to provide mutual emotional gratification and shared joy.

In a time when all family members spend large portions of each day outside the home, it is essential that some communication take place within the home to provide each other with emotional gratification and joy. Since the traditional functions of the family have been taken on by other institutions, if your family is not providing this mutual gratification and joy, it has no reason to exist.

Making your family a supportive and loving group does not require immense amounts of effort, but it does require time. You need to be there to hear about your child's basketball game, or to help her ride a bicycle, or to help him with his homework, so that your child will be there when you need his love or her support. You need to be there to reassure your spouse when she returns home exhausted after a business trip, or when he has had a frustrating day at work, so that he will be supportive of you when you need emotional strength, and she will be patient with you when you are under stress at the office. The amount of time you spend with your family will provide you with the confidence that results from knowing you are loved, and thus with the motivation and energy necessary to improve the other areas of your life. As a well-known motivational speaker told MDRT members:

> My number one priority, every single day, my top-dog priority in life, the foundation for which everything is built is to make certain I get up on the right side of the bed. Period! It's my top priority. When I have a headache. When I'm fighting off the flu—it's to make certain I'm on. This makes me better with my children (and let me tell you we still have our differences, but I'm better). I'm better with my wife, and I'm more creative when I write, I'm better when I'm in front of people. It sets the stage for everything I do!

As this speaker proves through example, a thoughtful and genuine love of your family can be the impetus you need to transform your attitude and thus improve your career, and it is one of the most natural and simple things you can do. A high-producer in the MDRT says:

> Being kind to others doesn't cost you any more breath than to blow out a candle. Wonderful things can happen when you say things like (to your wife) "I like your hair like that!" or (to your son) "thanks for helping me out that way, I really appreciate it." You are in a unique position to make people's

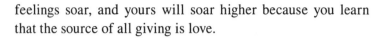
feelings soar, and yours will soar higher because you learn that the source of all giving is love.

To be able to give love and support to your family, you need to learn to interact with them in a positive way. One of the best ways to demonstrate love for your family is through a sense of humor. As a well-known writer explained to MDRT, a sense of humor means more than telling jokes or laughing at them, it means maximizing the impact of all the good things that happen in your life, and minimizing the impact of the negative. Any time people are intimately connected there will be times they hurt one another, sometimes intentionally and sometimes just through carelessness. To have a healthy and loving relationship with your family, it is necessary to accept the positive and the negative aspects of an intimate relationship with all family members. It is also true that in the family, as in society, change is constant. You have only 18 years to enjoy sharing your home with your children. As one motivational speaker says, when considering your family relationships it is vital to remember that "today is a once in a lifetime opportunity, a kaleidoscope of people and feelings and events that are coming together just this way once and it will never, ever, happen again."

Remember the advice of a renowned MDRT member, that the caring connection is the definition of success. Men and women, work and family are not separate entities, but they are integrated. When you make the decision to put your family first—to make them your primary focus in your life—the rewards in other areas of your life will be breathtaking. You will feel more comfortable accepting career and business challenges, and your confidence and genuine love for your family will reassure prospects that you can empathize with them and understand the dreams they have for their families. The power of a loving family can propel you to do greater things than you ever imagined possible.

Whole Person Success

The concept of whole person success has been proven to work for some of the most incredible salespeople in the world. Every salesperson, in fact, every person, wants to improve—to better his sales, to better her life, to lead the highest quality life possible. So why is there such a large group of people who never change their routines to make success possible? Many people are unaware that to attain true success it is necessary to change your entire life, not just a particular aspect of it. Your success in sales is directly related to your vision of yourself—to your educational and professional competence, to your good health, to your pride in and aid of your community, and to your positive and loving relationship with your family. As salespeople you have a weighty responsibility to yourself and to your prospects. You have one of the most essential careers in the world. As a top MDRT member says:

> Nothing significant happens in this world until someone starts the process by selling. Nothing happens until someone cares enough to try to sell someone else a product, a service, or an idea. We are all salespeople. We are all selling all of the time. We're selling ideas, we're selling answers to problems, we're selling all the value you can add. We're selling our ability to manage and mobilize and motivate. We're all selling, all of the time. But, and this is important, not just anyone can be a sales success.

In order to be a success in sales, you must be a success in life. You must push yourself to develop into the vision you have of a successful human being. You must struggle to expand your mind, to appreciate and value your relationships with your family, to give your body the attention it needs to be healthy, to repay your community for the business and the sense of belonging it has bestowed on you. When you have accomplished this, professional success is sure to follow.

Beware the trap of achieving a little and becoming satisfied with that. As one eloquent member of MDRT says:

There's one statement true of every person, which is that none of us has reached his or her full potential. Isn't this true? Wherever we are today, there is room for improvement. We can improve our relationship with loved ones. We can improve our business. We can improve our health and vitality. We can improve our relationship with God. We can get greater levels of fulfillment and peace of mind. We can contribute more value and more service to the world.

Success requires a commitment to constant self-evaluation and improvement. Your life as a successful sales person begins with a commitment to becoming a whole person—to living a life of significance, happiness, and fulfillment. Commit yourself now to improving your education, your family relationships, your health and your community service. Your sales will improve, but more importantly, the world will be a brighter place because of your contributions to it.

ABOUT CFP

 Founded in 1927 by the most successful financial planners in the nation, the Million Dollar Round Table is now an international organization, with over twenty thousand members worldwide. The Round Table is an exclusive organization, accepting only those producers in the top six percent of the financial planning industry. An emphasis on the whole person, including family time, time management, education, professional behavior, and motivation is shared with members every year in the MDRT Annual Meeting. Members gather to learn from one another and from world-renowned experts in the industry, at times spending up to 10 percent of their annual income to attend, demonstrating the loyalty they have to the association and the value they place upon the knowledge made available to them at the meeting.

The Center for Productivity is the Round Table's publishing branch, developing information provided in the rich MDRT archives into quality motivational, educational, and training products that assist insurance and financial planning professionals in reaching the highest level of productivity. Established in 1996, CFP publishes in print, as well as producing material on audiotape, videotape, and CD-ROM. In the past three years, CFP has created products on a number of timely and useful topics, including technology, office management, training, self-study, long-term care, and now prospecting, closing, and sales techniques.

This book series, a co-publishing agreement with John Wiley & Sons, marks the first time information from the MDRT archives has been available to a general audience. For more information on the Million Dollar Round Table and the Center for Productivity, call 1-800-TRY-MDRT, or look through our web site at www.mdrtcfp.org.

INDEX